A WORKBOOK FOR SELF-STUDY

READING & WRITING BURMESE

Learn to Read, Write and Pronounce Burmese Correctly

A Zun Mo and Angus Johnstone

TUTTLE Publishing

Tokyo | Rutland, Vermont | Singapore

"Books to Span the East and West"

Tuttle Publishing was founded in 1832 in the small New England town of Rutland, Vermont [USA]. Our core values remain as strong today as they were then—to publish best-in-class books which bring people together one page at a time. In 1948, we established a publishing office in Japan—and Tuttle is now a leader in publishing English-language books about the arts, languages and cultures of Asia. The world has become a much smaller place today and Asia's economic and cultural influence has grown. Yet the need for meaningful dialogue and information about this diverse region has never been greater. Over the past seven decades, Tuttle has published thousands of books on subjects ranging from martial arts and paper crafts to language learning and literature—and our talented authors, illustrators, designers and photographers have won many prestigious awards. We welcome you to explore the wealth of information available on Asia at www.tuttlepublishing.com.

Published by Tuttle Publishing, an imprint of Periplus Editions (HK) Ltd.

www.tuttlepublishing.com

Copyright © 2022 by Periplus Editions (HK) Ltd.

All rights reserved.

Library of Congress Catalog-in-Publication Data in progress

ISBN 978-0-8048-5262-3

Photo and illustration credits:
Inside front cover, Khukuklub, Wikimedia Commons. Page 86, Visual Intermezzo; page 89, Peacefully7; page 90, Rolf_52; page 92, PiggingFoto; page 94, Firstyahoo. All from Shutterstock.

Distributed by:

North America, Latin America and Europe
Tuttle Publishing
364 Innovation Drive, North Clarendon,
VT 05759-9436 USA.
Tel: 1(802) 773-8930 Fax: 1(802) 773-6993
info@tuttlepublishing.com
www.tuttlepublishing.com

Asia Pacific
Berkeley Books Pte. Ltd.
3 Kallang Sector #04-01, Singapore 349278
Tel: (65) 6741-2178 Fax: (65) 6741-2179
inquiries@periplus.com.sg
www.periplus.com

25 24 23 22   5 4 3 2 1   2201VP

Printed in Malaysia

TUTTLE PUBLISHING® is a registered trademark of Tuttle Publishing, a division of Periplus Editions (HK) Ltd.

Contents

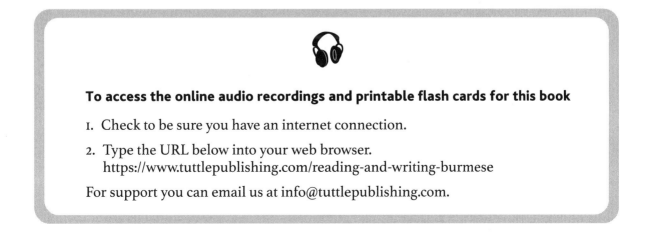

To access the online audio recordings and printable flash cards for this book

1. Check to be sure you have an internet connection.

2. Type the URL below into your web browser.
   https://www.tuttlepublishing.com/reading-and-writing-burmese

For support you can email us at info@tuttlepublishing.com.

How to Use This Book

Who is this book for?

This book is designed for learners of the Myanmar language who wish to learn to read and write using the Burmese alphabet. It is aimed at beginning-level students, and no prior knowledge of Burmese is required. It can be used by self-study students or in a classroom.

What is the purpose of this book?

The purpose of this book is to introduce the letters of the Burmese alphabet and to provide plentiful practice material so that students can learn the basics of reading and writing. The practice exercises in the book use words and phrases that are common in contemporary Myanmar, covering useful topics such as numbers, food and social media.

How is the book structured?

This book is divided into three main parts. **Part 1** introduces the 33 basic letters of the Burmese alphabet. Each letter is introduced with a mnemonic illustration to aid memorization of its sound and shape.

Part 2 introduces the 25 vowel sounds that can be added to the 33 basic letters to make syllables. Both Part 1 and Part 2 include handwriting boxes so that students can practice tracing the letter and writing it freehand, as well as exercises that allow students to practice reading and writing the letter as part of words and sentences.

Part 3 presents everyday Burmese vocabulary grouped into various useful subject categories, including daily expressions, numbers, food, computers and social media. As well as handwriting exercises, there are challenging and fun reading and writing activities. A key at the back of the book provides answers to all the exercises.

Online audio recordings are provided to accompany the sections of the book marked with a headphones logo, to help students learn the pronunciation of letters, syllables and words. Free downloadable flash cards help students learn the letters and vocabulary quickly. Audio recordings and downloadable flash cards can be accessed using the link on page 8.

An Overview of the Burmese Writing System

The Burmese writing system is composed of consonants and vowels, which are combined into syllables to spell out words. There are 33 letters in the basic Burmese alphabet (see chart on the inside front cover) and 32 of them are consonants. In addition, there are 25 additional symbols that represent vowels and medial consonants. Medial consonants are special characters that pair with consonants to modify how those consonants are read. For example, the medial consonant ya can be added to the letter ma to make the sound mya.

To be able to read Burmese script, you must learn both the consonants and the additions that represent vowels and medial consonants. Most Burmese vowels have three tones: high and short, low and level, and high and long. There is also a "stopped" tone which is high and very short It is possible to form a word with consonants only, but vowels alone cannot form a word.

A Brief History of the Burmese Language

Burmese belongs to the Sino-Tibetan language family, as do some of the languages of neighboring China, India, Thailand, and Nepal. It is the national language of Myanmar, spoken by the majority of the population either as a first or second language (there are also many other languages spoken in different regions of the country). The earliest recorded text in Burmese appears in the Myazedi (emerald stupa) stone inscription, which was written in four languages—Burmese, Pali, Mon and Pyu—in early twelfth century Bagan. Having been in close contact with Pali, the language of Theravāda Buddhism, several Pali words appear in Burmese. Burmese has also incorporated words from foreign languages including English and Hindi, so the learner may come across words that sound familiar, such as ကား karr (car) or အာလူး ar loo (potato).

Romanization, Pronunciation and Tones

This book uses the most common romanized system of Burmese, widely known as Myanglish or Burglish, which is Burmese written in its nearest equivalent using the Latin alphabet.

🎧 Consonants

Most of the romanized Burmese consonants are pronounced in the same way as their English equivalent. The consonants listed below can sometimes be tricky for non-native speakers.

Also note that final consonants in Burmese words are always silent. They are "swallowed" by briefly closing the back of the throat (this is known as a "glottal stop").

Myanglish	Pronunciation	Example
ng	like **ng** in singer	ငါး ngarr "fish" or "five"
ny	like **nio** in onion	ည nya "night"
t	like **t** in star (close to /d/ sound)	တစ် tit "one"
ht	like **t** in tart	ထီး htee "umbrella"
p	like **pp** in slipper	ပဲ peh "beans"
ph	like **p** in part	ဖား pharr "frog"
th	like **th** in there	သား tharr "son"

🎧 Vowels and tones

A tone is a variation in pitch when a word is pronounced. In Burmese, most vowels have three different tones; high and short; low and level; and high and long. There is also a "stopped" tone which is high and very short. A variation in the pitch or tone of a vowel changes the meaning of a word.

Word	Tone	Meaning
စ sa	high and short	start
စာ sar	low and level	letter
စား sarr	high and long	eat
စက် set	stopped	machine

Vowel tones in this book are represented by spellings that approximate English vowel length and pronunciation. An alphabetical list of those spellings is written below, with pronunciation guidelines. *An asterisk next to the English pronunciation example denotes that the final consonant of the English word should be swallowed in a glottal stop (see page 5), and not be audible.

🎧 Myanglish	Pronunciation	Example
a	like "art" in tart*	က ka dance
ae	like "e" in cherry	ဝယ် wae buy
aet	like "elp" in help*	နဲ့ naet and
ainq	like "int" in pint*	ချိုင့် chainq tiffin box
ai	like "ai" in Thailand	ဆိုင် sai shop
aii	like "ai" in Thai	ရိုင်း yaii rude
ain	like "ain" in rainy	စိန် sain diamond
aint	like "aint" in faint*	အမိန့် amaint order
an	like "an" in van*	ကန် kan lake
ann	like "and" in land*	လမ်း lann street
ant	like "ant" in ant*	လန့် lant shocked
ar	like "ar" in narcotics	ညာ nyar right
arr	like "arr" in car*	စား sarr eat
at	like "at" in mat*	ရပ် yat stop
ate	like "ate" in date*	ပိတ် pate close
aung	like "ound" in pound*	ကြောင် kyaung cat
aungg	like "ow" in now	ကျောင်း kyaungg school
aungt	like "ount" in count*	စောင့် saungt wait
aw	like "or" in or*	ကော် kaw glue
awt	like "ork" in pork*	သော့ thawt key

aww	like "aw" in saw	မော maww tired
ay	like "A" in ABC	ရေ yay water
ayt	like "ave" in cave*	မေ့ mayt forget
ayy	like "ay" in bay	ဆေး sayy medicine
ee	like "ee" in see	မီး mee fire
eet	like "eet" in beetroot	ထိ hteet touch
ein	like "ain" in gain*	သိမ်း thein keep
eh	like "air" in air*	ရဲ yeh police
et	like "et" in pet*	ခက် khet difficult
i	like "e" in reuse	နီ ni red
in	like "in" in basin*	ဆင် sin elephant
inn	like "in" in win*	ဟင်း hinn curry
int	like "ink" in sink*	သင့် thint should
it	like "it" in sit*	တစ် tit one
ite	like "ite" in bite*	ကြိုက် kyite like
o	like "o" in photo	ဟို ho that
ote	like "oat" in coat*	အလုပ် alote work
oh	like "ol" in sold*	မိုး moe rain
oht	like "o" in both*	နို့ noht milk
on	like "on" in online	မွန် mon Mon State
onn	like "on" in spoon	ဇွန်း zonn spoon
ont	like "ont" in continent	တွန့် tont shrink
oo	like "oo" in school	အရူး ayoo idiot
oot	like "oot" in shoot*	အခု akhoot now
out	like "out" in snout*	သောက် thout drink
'own	like "ow" in owner	ဖုန် phown dust
'ownn	like "ow" in own*	ဖုန်း phone phone
ownt	like "on't" in won't*	မုန့် m'ownt snack
u	like "u" in super	ပူ pu hot
ut	like "ut" in put*	လွတ် lut empty

Stacked letters

As a side note, you may sometimes find unusual "stacked letters" as you go along, such as in the word တိရစ္ဆာန် ta rit san (animal). Those stacked letters come from Pali and therefore the formation of the words is a bit more complicated.

When the letters are stacked together, the top letter is a vowel that pairs with the consonant immediately preceding it. The bottom letter is a consonant that is combined with the vowel that comes immediately after.

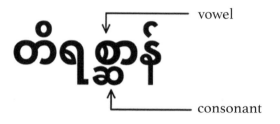

vowel

consonant

Punctuation

There are not a lot of punctuation marks in Burmese. One stroke (၊) denotes a comma (,) and two strokes (၊၊) at the end of a sentence denote a full stop (.) or question mark (?).

A note about names

Burma is the former name of Myanmar before 1989. The country's official name today is the Republic of the Union of Myanmar. However, some countries like the USA and the UK still use the name Burma. The office language of this country is Burmese. Therefore, the country is Myanmar and the language is Burmese.

To access the online audio recordings and printable flash cards for this book

1. Check to be sure you have an internet connection.

2. Type the URL below into your web browser.
   https://www.tuttlepublishing.com/reading-and-writing-burmese

For support you can email us at info@tuttlepublishing.com.

Part

Consonants

Burmese has 33 letters that are classified as consonants, usually in the form of initial consonant plus a, for example ka, sa, da, na, ba, etc.

In this section of the book you will find consonants with stroke order diagrams, boxes for tracing and writing practice, mnemonic illustrations to help you remember the letter, and audio files to model correct pronunciation of each consonant and vocabulary word.

Note that although the consonants ၺ ta, ၹ hta, ၮ da, ဎ da and ဠ la are usually displayed in standard charts of Burmese consonants, such as the chart on the inside front cover of this book, these letters are no longer used in modern Burmese. For that reason they have not been included in the reading and writing practice exercises in this book.

Note also that the basic vowel a is also included in these basic 33 letters.

Although this book uses the most common romanized system of Burmese, it is sometimes difficult to convey Burmese sounds accurately using the Roman alphabet, so use the romanization as a guide and refer to the online audio files (see page 8) for accurate pronunciation.

Consonant Formation Ka/Ga, Kha, Ga, Ga

 **Ka/Ga**

This is a sound in between ga and ka as in "scarf" and it can be pronounced as either.

a very long s<u>car</u>f

 Writing Tip: Ka/Ga has two strokes, but you don't need to remove your pen in between.

Trace these letters:

က	က	က	က	က	က	က	က	က	က	က	က	က	က

Write the letters in the boxes below. Then practice writing this letter in the blank space in each of the vocabulary words.

1. a ka (dance)

အ	

2. nya ga (last night)

ည	

3. ga zarr (to play)

	ဇား

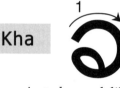 **Kha**

An aspirated sound, like "co" in "<u>co</u>lor"

a <u>co</u>lorful paint palette

 Writing Tip: Kha has one curved stroke.

Trace these letters:

ခ	ခ	ခ	ခ	ခ	ခ	ခ	ခ	ခ	ခ	ခ	ခ	ခ	ခ

Write the letters in the boxes below. Then practice writing this letter in the blank space in each of the vocabulary words.

1. la kha (salary)

လ	

2. kha na (for a moment)

	က

3. kha yee (trip)

	ရီး

Ga

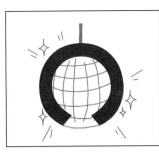

Like "ga" in "gala"

a mirror ball at the gala

✏️ **Writing Tip:** Ga has one curved stroke.

Trace these letters:

ဂ	ဂ	ဂ	ဂ	ဂ	ဂ	ဂ	ဂ	ဂ	ဂ	ဂ	ဂ	ဂ	ဂ

Write the letters in the boxes below. Then practice writing this letter in the blank space in each of the vocabulary words.

1. ga ga na na (precisely)

	ဃ		န		ဏ

2. nar ga (Naga tribe)

နာ	

3. ga nann (crab, numerical digit)

	ကန်း

....

Ga

Like "gar" in "garden"

flowers in a garden

✏️ **Writing Tip:** Ga has two strokes.

Trace these letters:

ဃ	ဃ	ဃ	ဃ	ဃ	ဃ	ဃ	ဃ	ဃ	ဃ	ဃ	ဃ	ဃ	ဃ

Write the letters in the boxes below. Then practice writing this letter in the blank space in the vocabulary word.

1. ga ga na na (precisely)

ဂ		န	ဏ

Nga

A nasalized sound made in the back of the throat. Sounds like the last four letters of "singer."

that guy is such a good si<u>nger</u>

✍ **Writing Tip:** Nga has one curved stroke.

Trace these letters:

Write the letters in the boxes below. Then practice writing this letter in the blank space in each of the vocabulary words.

1. nga pa li (Ngapali [beach resort])

2. nga yeh (hell)

Sa

Like "sa" in "<u>sa</u>lon." Sometimes it is pronounced za.

a <u>sa</u>lon hairdryer

✍ **Writing Tip:** Sa has two strokes.

Trace these letters:

Write the letters in the boxes below. Then practice writing this letter in the blank space in each of the vocabulary words.

1. a sa (beginning)

2. za garr (language)

3. sa nay nayt (Saturday)

Sa

Like "sa" in "sardine."

a can of sardines

✍ **Writing Tip:** Sa has two strokes. The first is curved and loops back on itself. The second is a full circle touching the side of the first.

Trace these letters:

သ	သ	သ	သ	သ	သ	သ	သ	သ	သ	သ	သ	သ	သ

Write the letters in the boxes below. Then practice writing this letter in the blank space in each of the vocabulary words.

1. sa yar (male teacher)

	ရ

2. sa yar ma (female teacher)

	ရ	မ

....

 Za

Like "za" in "Zara."

a Zara clothing tag

✍ **Writing Tip:** Za has one curved stroke that loops back on itself.

Trace these letters:

ဇ	ဇ	ဇ	ဇ	ဇ	ဇ	ဇ	ဇ	ဇ	ဇ	ဇ	ဇ	ဇ	ဇ

Write the letters in the boxes below. Then practice writing this letter in the blank space in each of the vocabulary words.

1. za nee (wife)

	နီး

2. za yarr (grid)

	ယား

3. za yar (old age)

	ရ

Za

<u>za</u>pped by the hairdryer

Like "za" in "<u>zap</u>"

✍ **Writing Tip:** Za has three strokes. First a full circle, then a small curve within the circle and finally a straight line which cuts back to meet the circle.

Trace these letters:

Write the letters in the boxes below. Note that there are no vocabulary words that use this consonant alone without a vowel addition.

....

Nya

please chop two <u>oni</u>ons

Like "nio" in "<u>oni</u>on"

✍ **Writing Tip:** Nya has two strokes. First, an almost-complete circle which curves away from itself to form a tail. Second, a curve matching the first which connects to its back.

Trace these letters:

Write the letters in the boxes below. Then practice writing this letter in the blank space in each of the vocabulary words.

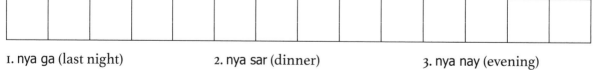

1. nya ga (last night)

2. nya sar (dinner)

3. nya nay (evening)

Revision

Circle the correct letter. Check your answers on page 96. Once you have checked your answers, practice writing the letter on the line provided. You can make the writing practice more challenging by covering the Burmese script!

1. sa   သ   စ   ဃ   ဆ   ခ   ....

2. ga   ဂ   ည   ဏ   ခ   င   ....

3. za   ည   င   ရ   ခ   ဏ   ....

4. kha   ည   သ   ရ   င   ခ   ....

5. nya   င   ဃ   သ   ဏ   ည   ....

6. ka   ည   စ   သ   ဏ   ရ   ....

7. nga   ရ   ခ   င   ဏ   ည   ....

8. ga   ဃ   ဆ   ဏ   ည   င   ....

9. sa   င   ခ   ဏ   ရ   ည   ....

10. za   စ   ဆ   ဏ   င   ဃ   ....

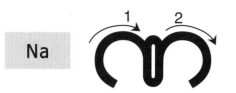

Consonant Formation — Na, Ta, Hta, Da

Na

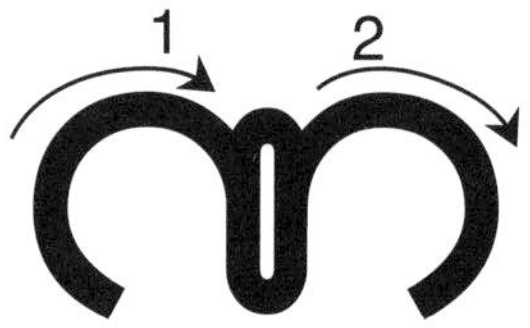

Like "nar" in "<u>nar</u>coleptic."

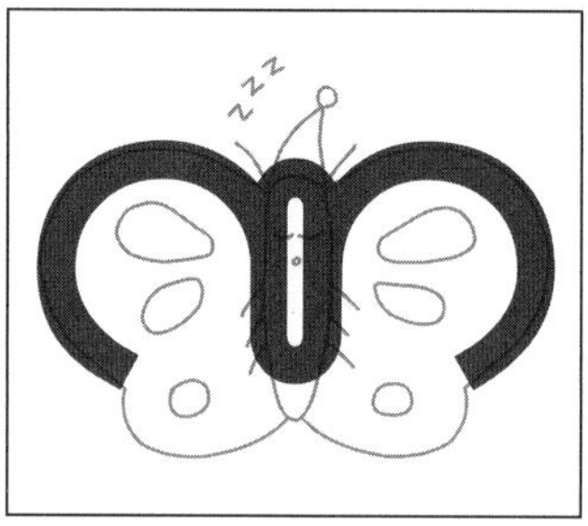

the <u>nar</u>coleptic butterfly is always asleep

Writing Tip: Na has two strokes. The middle oval-shaped section is completed in the first stroke. Then the second stroke is a symmetrical curve away from the oval.

Trace these letters:

န	န	န	န	န	န	န	န	န	န	န	န	န	န

Write the letters in the boxes below. Then practice writing this letter in the blank space in the vocabulary word.

1. kha na (one moment)

ခ	

Ta

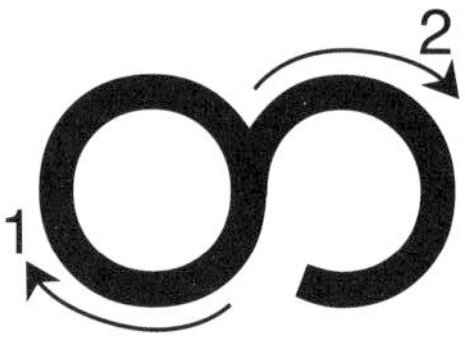

An aspirated sound, like "tar" in "s<u>tar</u>."

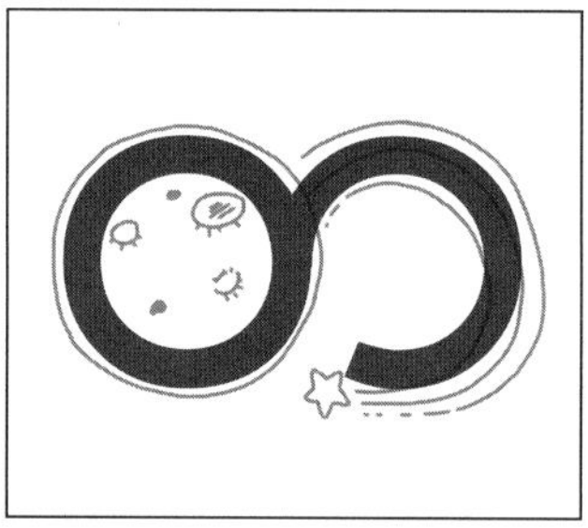

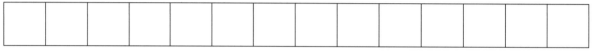

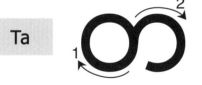

a s<u>tar</u> orbiting a moon

Writing Tip: Ta has two strokes.

Trace these letters:

တ	တ	တ	တ	တ	တ	တ	တ	တ	တ	တ	တ	တ	တ

Write the letters in the boxes below. Then practice writing this letter in the blank space in each of the vocabulary words.

1. ta mar (neem tree)

	မာ

2. ta larr (coffin)

	လား

3. ta yaww (violin)

	ယော

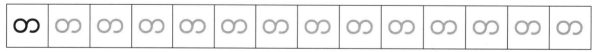

Hta

hot and cold water <u>taps</u>

An aspirated sound, like "ta" in "<u>tap</u>."

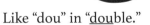 **Writing Tip:** Hta has two strokes.

Trace these letters:

∞	∞	∞	∞	∞	∞	∞	∞	∞	∞	∞	∞	∞	∞

Write the letters in the boxes below. Then practice writing this letter in the blank space in each of the vocabulary words.

ɪ. Hta par! (Stand up!)

	ပါ

2. hta minn (cooked rice)

	မင်း

. . . .

 Da

<u>dat</u>'s a sideways "w"

Like "dou" in "<u>double</u>."

 **Writing Tip:** Da has one stroke.

Trace these letters:

ဒ	ဒ	ဒ	ဒ	ဒ	ဒ	ဒ	ဒ	ဒ	ဒ	ဒ	ဒ	ဒ	ဒ

Write the letters in the boxes below. Then practice writing this letter in the blank space in each of the vocabulary words.

ɪ. da tha ma (tenth)

	သ	မ

2. da gar (generous donor)

	ကာ

Consonants **17**

Da

Like "dar" in "<u>dar</u>k."

it gets <u>dar</u>k when the sun sets

👆 **Writing Tip:** Da has one stroke. The inside curve comes at the end.

Trace these letters:

Write the letters in the boxes below. Then practice writing this letter in the blank space in each of the vocabulary words.

1. da na (wealth)

2. da layt (custom)

3. da neet (nipa palm frond)

Na

Like "na" in "<u>na</u>h."

<u>Na</u>h, it's not a snake...

👆 **Writing Tip:** Na has one stroke.

Trace these letters:

Write the letters in the boxes below. Then practice writing this letter in the blank space in each of the vocabulary words.

1. na garr (dragon)

2. mar na (arrogance)

3. na wa ma (ninth)

Pa

Like "pa" in "<u>Pa</u>pa."

my <u>pa</u>pa has a big nose

✍ **Writing Tip:** Pa has one stroke.

Trace these letters:

Write the letters in the boxes below. Then practice writing this letter in the blank space in each of the vocabulary words.

1. pa hta ma (first)

∞ ⊌

2. pa war (shawl)

ဝါ

3. pa yinn (amber)

ယင်း

....

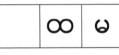

Pha

An aspirated sound, like "pa" in "<u>pa</u>rk."

there's a parrot in this <u>pa</u>rk

✍ **Writing Tip:** Pha has one stroke.

Trace these letters:

Write the letters in the boxes below. Then practice writing this letter in the blank space in each of the vocabulary words.

1. pha larr
(Myanmar decorative silver bowl)

လား

2. tharr a pha (father and son)

သား | အ |

3. kyet pha (rooster)

Ba

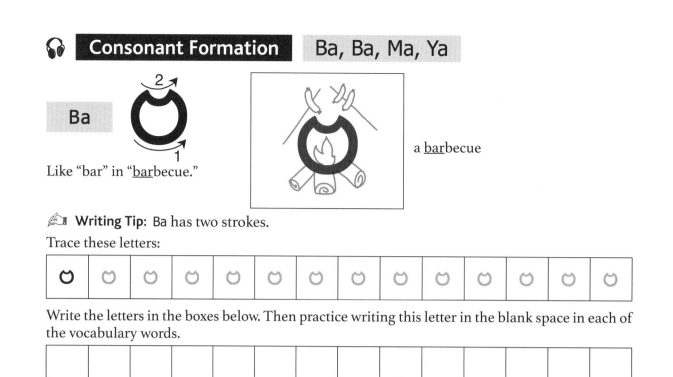

Like "bar" in "<u>bar</u>becue."

a <u>bar</u>becue

✍ **Writing Tip:** Ba has two strokes.

Trace these letters:

Write the letters in the boxes below. Then practice writing this letter in the blank space in each of the vocabulary words.

ɪ. ba la (big muscles)   2. ba mar za garr (Burmese language)   3. ba li (mosque)

Ba

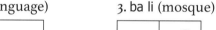

Like "ba" in "<u>bar</u>."

leave your empty glasses on the <u>bar</u>

✍ **Writing Tip:** Ba has two strokes.

Trace these letters:

Write the letters in the boxes below. Then practice writing this letter in the blank space in each of the vocabulary words.

ɪ. a ba (uncle; parent's elder brother)   2. meet ba (parents)   3. ba wa (life)

Ma

Like "ma" in "Mama."

my <u>ma</u>ma has a funny nose

✍ Writing Tip: Ma has two strokes.

Trace these letters:

 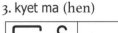

Write the letters in the boxes below. Then practice writing this letter in the blank space in each of the vocabulary words. Note the use of the two lines denoting the Burmese full stop in number 2.

1. a ma (elder sister)

အစ်	

2. Ma ka boo. (I don't dance.)

	က	ဘူး॥

3. kyet ma (hen)

ကြက်	

. . . .

Ya

Like "ya" in "yarn."

two balls of <u>ya</u>rn

✍ Writing Tip: Ya has one stroke.

Trace these letters:

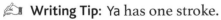

Write the letters in the boxes below. Then practice writing this letter in the blank space in the vocabulary word.

ya ma kar (beverage)

🎧 **Consonant Formation**   Ya, La, Wa, Tha

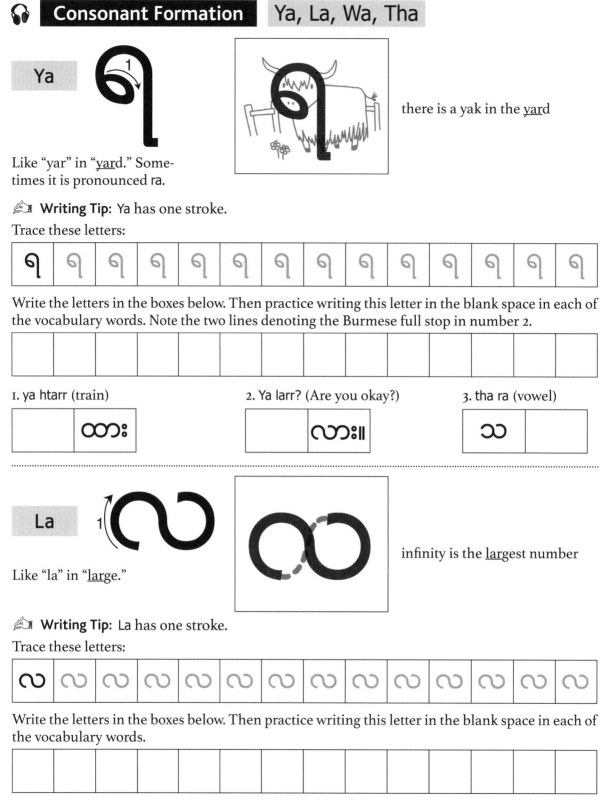

Ya

there is a yak in the <u>yar</u>d

Like "yar" in "<u>yar</u>d." Sometimes it is pronounced ra.

✍ **Writing Tip:** Ya has one stroke.

Trace these letters:

Write the letters in the boxes below. Then practice writing this letter in the blank space in each of the vocabulary words. Note the two lines denoting the Burmese full stop in number 2.

1. ya htarr (train)

2. Ya larr? (Are you okay?)

3. tha ra (vowel)

La

infinity is the <u>larg</u>est number

Like "la" in "<u>larg</u>e."

✍ **Writing Tip:** La has one stroke.

Trace these letters:

Write the letters in the boxes below. Then practice writing this letter in the blank space in each of the vocabulary words.

1. di la (this month)

2. a la karr (free of charge)

3. ngarr la (five months)

22 PART ONE

Wa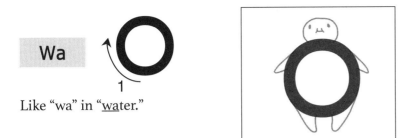

Like "wa" in "<u>wa</u>ter."

in Myanmar "<u>wa</u>" means "fat"

✍ **Writing Tip:** Wa has one stroke. There is a small gap at the top and bottom of ◯ wa in some computer fonts, but when written by hand, it is just a circle, without any gaps.

Trace these letters:

Write the letters in the boxes below. Then practice writing this letter in the blank space in each of the vocabulary words.

1. ma wa boo (not fat)

2. tha bar wa (natural)

....

Tha

Like "tha" in "<u>Thar</u> she blows!"

"<u>Thar</u> she blows!"

✍ **Writing Tip:** Tha has two strokes.

Trace these letters:

Write the letters in the boxes below. Then practice writing this letter in the blank space in each of the vocabulary words.

1. tha mee (daughter)

2. tha yeh (ghost)

3. tha bar wa (natural)

Ha

"Ha ha ha!"

Like "ha" in "<u>ha ha</u>."

 Writing Tip: Ha has two strokes.

Trace these letters:

ဟ	ဟ	ဟ	ဟ	ဟ	ဟ	ဟ	ဟ	ဟ	ဟ	ဟ	ဟ	ဟ	ဟ

Write the letters in the boxes below. Note that there are no vocabulary words that use this consonant alone without a vowel addition.

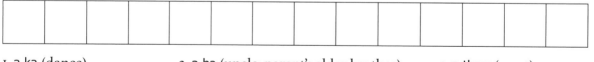

....

Ah

an <u>art</u>y 3 with a tail

Like "ah" in "<u>ar</u>t."

 Writing Tip: Ah has two strokes.

Trace these letters:

အ	အ	အ	အ	အ	အ	အ	အ	အ	အ	အ	အ	အ	အ

Write the letters in the boxes below. Then practice writing this letter in the blank space in each of the vocabulary words.

1. a ka (dance)

2. a ba (uncle; parent's elder brother)

3. a tharr (meat)

Circle the correct letter. Check your answer on page 96. Once you have checked your answers, practice writing the letter on the line provided. You can make the writing practice more challenging by covering the Burmese script!

1. nya ည်   ည   ၡ   ရ   ဒ   ....

2. ya ဒ   လ   ရ   မ   ၡ   ....

3. kha ဃ   ခ   ()   ဒ   ဝ   ....

4. ma ပ   မ   ဖ   က   ဖ   ....

5. hta ထ   သ   ထ   သ   ဃ   ....

6. tha သ   ဃ   ထ   သ   ထ   ....

7. ta ဃ   ထ   ထ   သ   သ   ....

8. na ည်   ရ   ၡ   ည   လ   ....

9. ah သ   အ   ဒ   ထ   သ   ....

10. la ဃ   ဃ   ထ   ထ   လ   ....

11. pa ပ   က   ()   ဖ   ဝ   ....

12. ka ဃ   ထ   ဃ   လ   သ   ....

Part

Vowels

Burmese is a tonal language, and most vowels have three different tones: high and short; low and level; and high and long. There is also a "stopped" tone which is high and very short. A variation in the tone of a vowel changes the meaning of a word.

In this section you will learn how to read and write all the vowel tones, and how they attach to the consonants learned in Part 1. Note that although most of the characters in this section are classified as vowels, many of them are romanized with a consonant at the end in order to convey the tone. Use the romanization as a guideline, and listen to the online audio files (see page 8) to hear correct pronunciation of each tone.

In this section you will also learn other characters that modify the consonant sounds you learned in Part 1, including medial consonants and aspirated sounds.

In this section, for every new vowel addition, there is a tracing exercise showing examples of vowels when added to a consonant. Note that this tracing exercise does not show every possible vowel combination, just a selection of examples to help you see how the vowel attaches to a consonant.

—	a as in t<u>a</u>rt (short tone)
_ɔ or _ɂ	ar as in n<u>a</u>rcotics (middle tone)
_ɔː or _ɂː	arr as in c<u>ar</u> (long tone)

Above are the standard vowel additions for a, ar and arr. Note that there is no addition required for a, the shortest tone, as it is the default for all consonants.

However, if some consonants are joined by the vowel _ɔ to produce a longer tone, they will end up looking like a different consonant. For example, if ပ was joined by _ɔ it would become တ, which looks like the consonant တ ta. For this reason, for the consonants ခ, ဂ, င, ဒ, ပ and ဝ we use the versions of a, ar and arr on the second row, above. To form this vowel, the above additions are written to the right of the consonant.

Practice tracing the example vowel and consonant combinations.

က	ကာ	ကား		ဆ	ဆာ	ဆား		ထ	ထာ	ထား		ည	ညာ	ညား
ka	kar	karr		sa	sar	sarr		hta	htar	htarr		nya	nyar	nyarr

န	နာ	နား		မ	မာ	မား		ရ	ရာ	ရား		အ	အာ	အား
na	nar	narr		ma	mar	marr		ya	yar	yarr		a	ar	arr

ခ	ခါ	ခါး		ဂ	ဂါ	ဂါး		င	ငါ	ငါး
kha	khar	kharr		ga	gar	garr		nga	ngar	ngarr

ဒ	ဒါ	ဒါး		ပ	ပါ	ပါး		ဝ	ဝါ	ဝါး
da	dar	darr		pa	par	parr		wa	war	warr

Practice reading these words that contain a, ar, or arr vowels. Trace the gray letters then practice writing them freehand. You can challenge yourself further by writing the whole word.

1. sayarma   female teacher

   ဆရာမ ....

2. ngarr   fish, five

   ငါး ....

3. a sarr a sar   food

   အစားအစာ ....

4. karr sa yar   driver

   ကားဆရာ ....

5. a ya thar   flavor

   အရသာ ....

6. a tharr   meat

   အသား ....

7. Arr larr?   Are you free?

   အားလား။ ....

8. pa war   shawl

   ပဝါ ....

9. ya htarr   train

   ရထား ....

🎧 Vowel Formation Eet, I, Ee

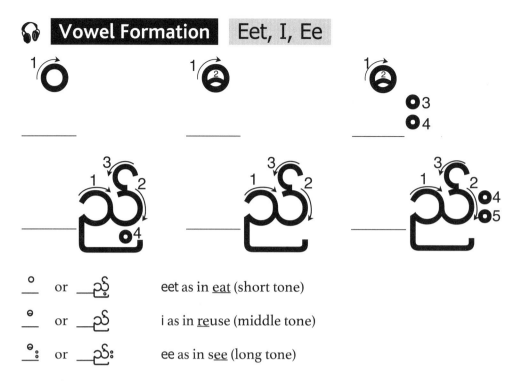

° —	or	___ ည့်	eet as in <u>eat</u> (short tone)
⊖ —	or	___ ည်	i as in <u>reuse</u> (middle tone)
⊖ —:	or	___ ည်း	ee as in s<u>ee</u> (long tone)

To form this vowel, the additions in the first row above are written on top of the consonant (and to the right for the long tone), and the additions in the second row are written to the right of the consonant. Certain words are habitually used with one or other of these vowels. You can see some common usage examples in the writing exercise on page 31.

Practice tracing the example vowel and consonant combinations.

စိ	စိ	စီး	တိ	တိ	တီး	ဒိ	ဒိ	ဒီး	နိ	နိ	နီး
seet	si	see	teet	ti	tee	deet	di	dee	neet	ni	nee

ဘိ	ဘိ	ဘီး	မိ	မိ	မီး	ရိ	ရိ	ရီး	ဟိ	ဟိ	ဟီး
beet	bi	bee	meet	mi	mee	yeet	yi	yee	heet	hi	hee

စည့်	စည်	စည်း	ညည့်	ညည်	ညည်း	တည့်	တည်	တည်း
seet	si	see	nyeet	nyi	nyee	teet	ti	tee

ထည့်	ထည်	ထည်း	နည့်	နည်	နည်း	မည့်	မည်	မည်း
hteet	hti	htee	neet	ni	nee	meet	mi	mee

ရည့်	ရည်	ရည်း	သည့်	သည်	သည်း
yeet	yi	yee	theet	thi	thee

Practice reading these words that contain eet, i, or ee vowels. Trace the gray letters then practice writing them freehand. You can challenge yourself further by writing the whole word.

1. <u>htee</u>   umbrella

    ထီး

2. a <u>thee</u>   fruit

    အသီး

3. <u>meet</u> ba   parent

    မိဘ

4. kha <u>yee</u>   trip

    ခရီး

5. <u>Theet</u> larr?   Do you know?

    သိလား။

6. nar <u>yi</u>   clock, watch

    နာရီ

7. <u>yee</u> sarr   boyfriend, girlfriend

    ရည်းစား

8. <u>nyi</u> ma   little sister

    ညီမ

9. <u>Nee</u> larr?   Is it close?

    နီးလား။

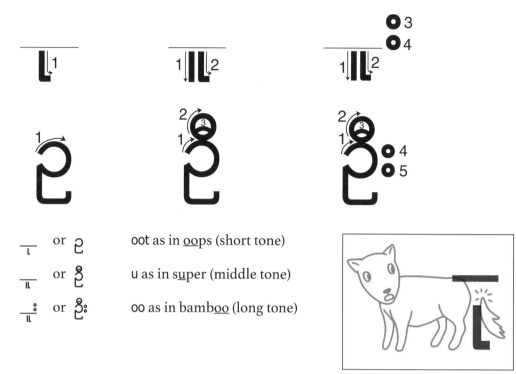

— or ᝰ	oot as in <u>oo</u>ps (short tone)	
— or ᝰ	u as in s<u>u</u>per (middle tone)	
— or ᝰ	oo as in bamb<u>oo</u> (long tone)	

Oops! The dog's tail is broken

To form this vowel, the additions on the first row are written below the consonant (and to the right for the long tone). On the second row is the standalone version of oot, u and oo; this version is never attached to a consonant, and is rarely used. It is only seen in some specific words, such as the honorific U that is given to older men to show respect, and yar thi oot toot (weather), see facing page, number 9.

Practice tracing the example vowel and consonant combinations.

koot	ku	koo	soot	su	soo	toot	tu	too	htoot	htu	htoo
noot	nu	noo	poot	pu	poo	phoot	phu	phoo	moot	mu	moo
yoot	yu	yoo	loot	lu	loo	thoot	thu	thoo	hoot	hu	hoo

🎧 **Reading and Writing Practice**   Oot, U, Oo

Practice reading these words that contain oot, u, or oo vowels. Trace the gray letters then practice writing them freehand. You can challenge yourself further by writing the whole word.

1. <u>tu</u>   chopsticks, hammer, nephew

   တူ ....

2. a <u>ku</u> a nyi   help

   အကူအညီ ....

3. ar <u>loo</u>   potato

   အာလူး ....

4. a <u>tu</u> <u>tu</u>   together

   အတူတူ ....

5. Ma theet <u>boo</u>.   I don't know.

   မသိဘူး။ ....

6. mee <u>pu</u>   iron (for smoothing clothes)

   မီးပူ ....

7. a <u>yoo</u>   crazy; idiot

   အရူး ....

8. meet tharr <u>soot</u>   family

   မိသားစု ....

9. yar thi <u>oot</u> <u>toot</u>   weather

   ရာသီဥတု ....

🎧 Vowel Formation Ayt, Ay, Ayy

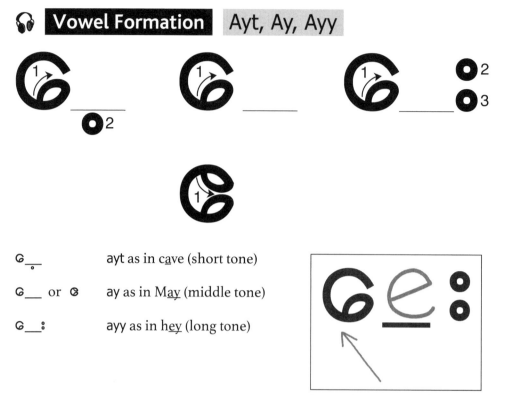

ၐ__	ayt as in c<u>a</u>ve (short tone)
ၐ__ or ၔ	ay as in M<u>ay</u> (middle tone)
ၐ__း	ayy as in h<u>ey</u> (long tone)

Hey! That e is upside down!

To form this vowel, use the additions as shown in the first row above. Beneath the first row is the standalone version of **ay**, the second tone. No consonants are needed for the version below. This version is never attached to a consonant, and is rarely used. It can only be seen in very specific words like Ayeyarwaddy (the name of the river).

Practice tracing the example vowel and consonant combinations.

ကေ့	ကေ	ကေး	ၐၚ	ၐၚ	ၐၚး	ၐတ	ၐတ	ၐတး
kayt	kay	kayy	ngayt	ngay	ngayy	tayt	tay	tayy

ၐန	ၐန	ၐနး	ၐပ	ၐပ	ၐပး	ၐဖ	ၐဖ	ၐဖး
nayt	nay	nayy	payt	pay	payy	phayt	phay	phayy

ၐမ	ၐမ	ၐမး	ၐယ	ၐယ	ၐယး	ၐရ	ၐရ	ၐရး
mayt	may	mayy	yayt	yay	yayy	yayt	yay	yayy

ၐလ	ၐလ	ၐလး	ၐဝ	ၐဝ	ၐဝး	ၐသ	ၐသ	ၐသး
layt	lay	layy	wayt	way	wayy	thayt	thay	thayy

Practice reading these words that contain ayt, ay, or ayy vowels. Trace the gray letters then practice writing them freehand. You can challenge yourself further by writing the whole word.

1. <u>yay</u>   water

   ‌ရေ ....

2. ka <u>layy</u>   baby

   ကလေး ....

3. nya <u>nay</u>   evening

   ညနေ ....

4. nya <u>zayy</u>   night market

   ညဈေး ....

5. <u>Ay</u> yar wa ti   Ayeyarwaddy (name of river)

   ဧရာဝတီ ....

6. <u>phay</u> <u>phay</u>   dad

   ဖေဖေ ....

7. <u>may</u> <u>may</u>   mom

   မေမေ ....

8. sar <u>yayy</u>   to write

   စာရေး ....

9. <u>mayy</u> <u>sayt</u>   chin

   မေးစေ့ ....

Vowel Formation   Aet, Ae, Eh

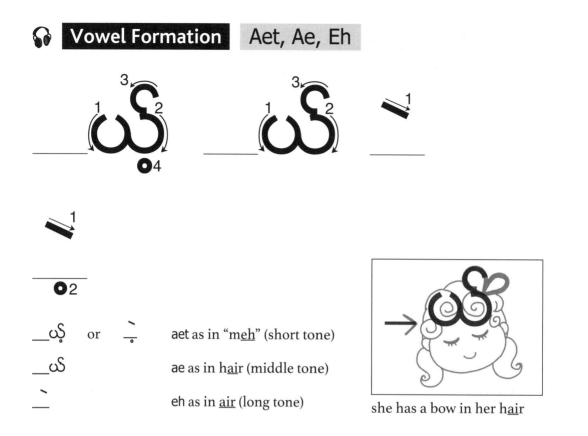

__ယ့်	or ◌ဲ့	aet as in "m<u>eh</u>" (short tone)
__ယ်		ae as in h<u>ai</u>r (middle tone)
`◌ဲ`		eh as in <u>air</u> (long tone)

she has a bow in her h<u>ai</u>r

To form this vowel, use the additions as shown above. Any consonant can be joined by any of the above vowels.

Practice tracing the example vowel and consonant combinations.

ကယ့်	ကယ်	ကဲ	ဆယ့်	ဆယ်	ဆဲ	ဇယ့်	ဇယ်	ဇဲ
kaet	kae	keh	saet	sae	seh	zaet	zae	zeh

တယ့်	တယ်	တဲ	နယ့်	နယ်	နဲ	ဖယ့်	ဖယ်	ဖဲ
taet	tae	teh	naet	nae	neh	phaet	phae	pheh

ခဲ့	ခယ်	ခဲ	ငယ့်	ငယ်	ငဲ	စဲ့	စယ်	စဲ	ပယ့်	ပယ်	ပဲ
khaet	khae	kheh	ngaet	ngae	ngeh	saet	sae	seh	paet	pae	peh

မဲ့	မယ်	မဲ	ရဲ့	ရယ်	ရဲ
maet	mae	meh	yaet	yae	yeh

Practice reading these words that contain aet, ae, or eh vowels. Trace the gray letters then practice writing them freehand. You can challenge yourself further by writing the whole word.

1. <u>yeh</u>   police

ရဲ ....

2. pha <u>yeh</u> thee   watermelon

ဖရဲသီး ....

3. a <u>meh</u> tharr   beef

အမဲသား ....

4. <u>beh</u> oot   duck egg

ဘဲဥ ....

5. tha <u>yeh</u>   ghost

သရဲ ....

6. nga <u>yeh</u>   hell

ငရဲ ....

7. yay <u>kheh</u>   ice

ရေခဲ ....

8. a <u>hteh</u>   in

အထဲ ....

9. a <u>lae</u>   middle

အလယ် ....

You should now be able to read the words below. Cover the right-hand column of text so you can only see the Burmese script on the left-hand side of the page. Try reading each Burmese word aloud and then uncover the column on the right to check. Keep practicing until you can read them all. For an extra challenge see if you can remember the English meaning before checking.

ဆရာမ — sa yar ma (female teacher)

ငါး — ngarr (fish, five)

အစားအစာ — a sarr a sar (food)

ကားဆရာ — karr sa yar (driver)

အရသာ — a ya thar (flavor)

အသား — a tharr (meat)

အားလား။ — Arr larr? (Are you free?)

ပဝါ — pa war (shawl)

ရထား — ya htarr (train)

ထီး — htee (umbrella)

အသီး — a thee (fruit)

မိဘ — meet ba (parent)

ခရီး — kha yee (trip)

သိလား။ — Theet larr? (Do you know?)

နာရီ — nar yi (clock, watch)

ရည်းစား — yee sarr (boyfriend, girlfriend)

ညီမ — nyi ma (little sister)

နီးလား။ — Nee larr? (Is it close?)

တူ — tu (chopsticks, hammer, nephew)

အကူအညီ — a ku a nyi (help)

အာလူး — ar loo (potato)

အတူတူ — a tu tu (together)

မသိဘူး။ — Ma theet boo. (I don't know.)

မီးပူ	mee pu (iron [for smoothing clothes])
အရူး	a yoo (crazy; idiot)
မိသားစု	meet tharr soot (family)
ရာသီဥတု	yar thi oot toot (weather)
ရေ	yay (water)
ကလေး	ka layy (baby)
ညနေ	nya nay (evening)
ညဈေး	nya zayy (night market)
ဧရာဝတီ	Ay yar wa ti (Ayeyarwaddy)
ဖေဖေ	phay phay (dad)
မေမေ	may may (mom)
စာရေး	sar yayy (to write)
မေးစေ့	mayy sayt (chin)
ရဲ	yeh (police)
ဖရဲသီး	pha yeh thee (watermelon)
အမဲသား	a meh tharr (beef)
ဘဲဥ	beh oot (duck egg)
သရဲ	tha yeh (ghost)
ငရဲ	nga yeh (hell)
ရေခဲ	yay kheh (ice)
အထဲ	a hteh (in)
အလယ်	a lae (middle)

Vowel Formation Awt, Aw, Aww

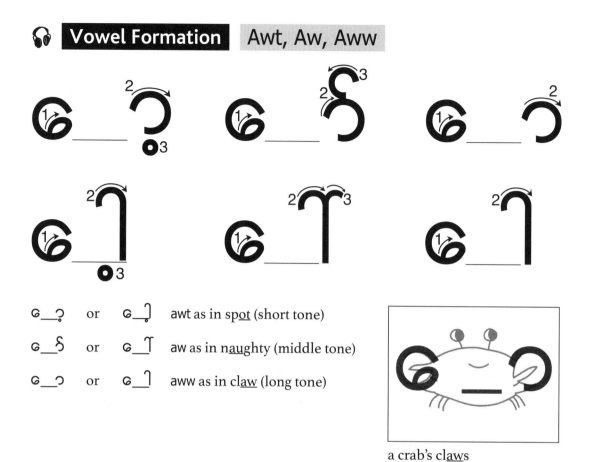

ေ‌ာ့	or	ေ‌ါ့	awt as in sp<u>o</u>t (short tone)
ေ‌ာ်	or	ေ‌ါ်	aw as in n<u>augh</u>ty (middle tone)
ေ‌ာ	or	ေ‌ါ	aww as in cl<u>aw</u> (long tone)

a crab's cl<u>aw</u>s

Above are the standard vowel additions for awt, aw and aww. The additions in the second line are used with the consonants ခ, ဂ, င, ဒ, ပ and ဝ to avoid confusion.

Practice tracing the example vowel and consonant combinations.

ကော့	ကော်	ကော	စော့	စော်	စော	တော့	တော်	တော
kawt	kaw	kaww	sawt	saw	saww	tawt	taw	taww

နော့	နော်	နော	မော့	မော်	မော	ရော့	ရော်	ရော
nawt	naw	naww	mawt	maw	maww	yawt	yaw	yaww

ခေါ့	ခေါ်	ခေါ	ဂေါ့	ဂေါ်	ဂေါ	ငေါ့	ငေါ်	ငေါ
khawt	khaw	khaww	gawt	gaw	gaww	ngawt	ngaw	ngaww

ဒေါ့	ဒေါ်	ဒေါ	ပေါ့	ပေါ်	ပေါ	ဝေါ့	ဝေါ်	ဝေါ
dawt	daw	daww	pawt	paw	paww	wawt	waw	waww

Practice reading these words that contain awt, aw, or aww vowels. Trace the gray letters then practice writing them freehand. You can challenge yourself further by writing the whole word.

1. <u>thawt</u> key

   ေသာ့

2. <u>kaw</u> <u>zaww</u> carpet

   ေကာ်ေဇာ

3. <u>maww</u> tae tired

   ေမာတယ်

4. <u>daww</u> tha anger

   ေဒါသ

5. a <u>daw</u> aunt

   အေဒါ်

6. <u>saww</u> <u>saww</u> early

   ေစာေစာ

7. a <u>paw</u> on

   အေပါ်

8. ta <u>yaww</u> violin

   တေယာ

9. <u>taww</u> thu country bumpkin girl

   ေတာသူ

🎧 **Vowel Formation**   Ant, An, Ann

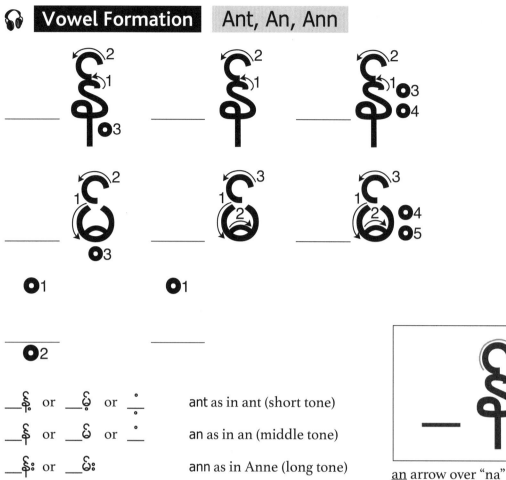

__ᢌᢜ or __ᢍ or ੍   ant as in ant (short tone)

__ᢌᢝ or __ᢎ or ੍   an as in an (middle tone)

__ᢌᢝး or __ᢎး   ann as in Anne (long tone)

an arrow over "na"

To form this vowel, use the additions as shown above. Any consonant can be joined by any of the above versions of ant, an or ann.

Practice tracing the example vowel and consonant combinations.

ကန့်	ကန်	ကန်း	ငန့်	ငန်	ငန်း	တန့်	တန်	တန်း
kant	kan	kann	ngant	ngan	ngann	tant	tan	tann

ပန့်	ပန်	ပန်း	စမ့်	စမ်	စမ်း	ထမ့်	ထမ်	ထမ်း
pant	pan	pann	sant	san	sann	htant	htan	htann

ဖမ့်	ဖမ်	ဖမ်း	လမ့်	လမ်	လမ်း	ခံ့	ခံ	င့်
phant	phan	phann	lant	lan	lann	khant	khan	ngant

ငံ	ညံ့	ညံ	နံ့	နံ	ရံ့	ရံ	အံ့	အံ
ngan	nyant	nyan	nant	nan	yant	yan	ant	an

🎧 **Reading and Writing Practice** Ant, An, Ann

Practice reading these words that contain ant, an, or ann vowels. Trace the gray letters then practice writing them freehand. You can challenge yourself further by writing the whole word.

1. <u>lann</u>   street

   လမ်း ....

2. a <u>khann</u>   room

   အခန်း ....

3. a <u>tann</u>   class

   အတန်း ....

4. <u>pann</u> thee   apple

   ပန်းသီး ....

5. <u>ngan</u> tae   salty

   ငန်တယ် ....

6. nan <u>yan</u>   wall

   နံရံ ....

7. a <u>yann</u>   very

   အရမ်း ....

8. kha <u>yann</u> thee   eggplant

   ခရမ်းသီး ....

9. a <u>khann</u> a <u>narr</u>   ceremony

   အခမ်းအနား ....

🎧 **Vowel Formation** Oht, O, Oh

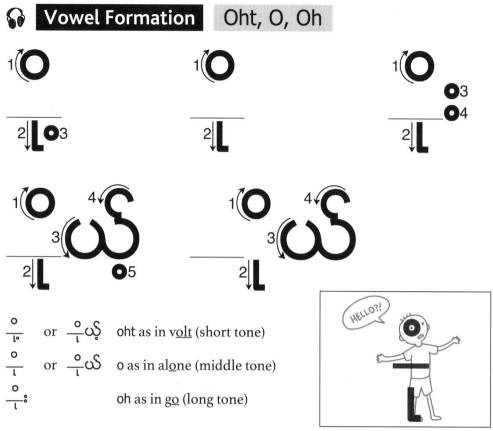

$\frac{o}{l_o}$ or $\frac{o}{l}$ ယ်	oht as in v<u>o</u>lt (short tone)	
$\frac{o}{l}$ or $\frac{o}{l}$ ယ်	o as in al<u>o</u>ne (middle tone)	
$\frac{o}{l}$ ႊ	oh as in g<u>o</u> (long tone)	

the thin man is al<u>o</u>ne

To form this vowel, use the additions as shown above. Any consonant can be joined by any of the above versions of oht, o or oh.

*Note in the chart below that for the vowels nyoht, nyo and nyoh the "leg" is on the right-hand side and not underneath as shown in the diagrams above. Computer fonts always have the "leg" on the right-hand side rather than underneath, but you can write it either way by hand.

Practice tracing the example vowel and consonant combinations.

ကို	ကို	ကို	ခို	ခို	ခို	ဆို	ဆို	ဆို	ညို	ညို	ညို
koht	ko	koh	khoht	kho	khoh	soht	so	soh	nyoht	nyo	nyoh

တို	တို	တို	ဒို	ဒို	ဒို	နို	နို	နို	ဖို	ဖို	ဖို
toht	to	toh	doht	do	doh	noht	no	noh	phoht	pho	phoh

မို	မို	မို	သို	သို	သို	ဟို	ဟို	ဟို	ကိုယ်	ကိုယ်
moht	mo	moh	thoht	tho	thoh	hoht	ho	hoh	koht	ko

🎧 Reading and Writing Practice Oht, O, Oh

Practice reading these words that contain oht, o, or oh vowels. Trace the gray letters then practice writing them freehand. You can challenge yourself further by writing the whole word.

1. kho pigeon

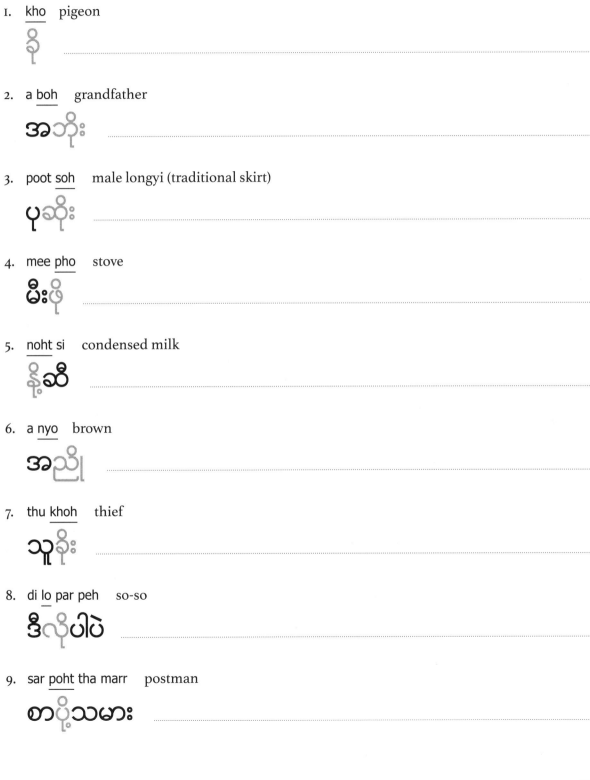

2. a boh grandfather

3. poot soh male longyi (traditional skirt)

4. mee pho stove

5. noht si condensed milk

6. a nyo brown

7. thu khoh thief

8. di lo par peh so-so

9. sar poht tha marr postman

🎧 Medial Consonant   Ya

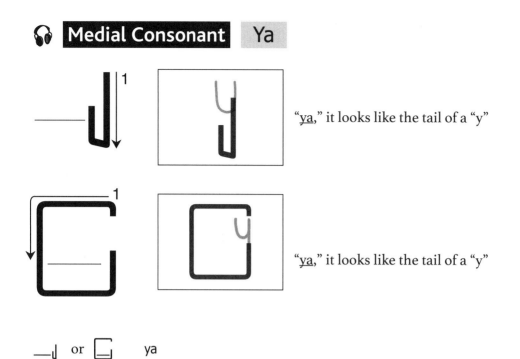

"ya," it looks like the tail of a "y"

"ya," it looks like the tail of a "y"

—◢ or ◣   ya

 Medial consonants are special characters that pair with consonants to modify how those consonants are read. For example, the medial consonant ya can be added to the letter ma to make the sound mya. Above are the medial consonant additions for ya. Either of the above additions can be used with consonants alone or consonants and vowels together, to form different tones. When ya is added to က ka or ခ kha, the pronunciation becomes kya or cha respectively (the romanization of the sounds found in "jar" or "charcoal"). See the letters marked with an asterisk.

*Note in the chart below that when ya is added to vowels that have a "leg" underneath, such as oot, u, oo or oht, o, oh, the "leg" goes to the right-hand side of the letter to provide more space for the ya.

Practice tracing the example vowel and consonant combinations.

ကျ	ကျာ	ကျား	ကျို	ကျိ	ကျီး	ချ	ချာ	ချား
kya*	kyar	kyarr	kyeet	kyi	kyee	cha*	char	charr

ကျေ.	ကျေ	ကျေး	ကျဲ.	ကျယ်	ကျဲ	ကျော့	ကျော်	ကျော
kyayt	kyay	kyayy	kyaet	kyae	kyeh	kyawt	kyaw	kyaww

ကျီ	ကျိ	ကျီး	ပြ	ပြိ	ပြီး	မျူ	မျု	မျူ
kyeet	kyi	kyee	pyeet	pyi	pyee	myoot	myu	myoo

မြန့်	မြန်	မြန်း	ဖျော့	ဖျော်	ဖျော	ပျို.	ပျို	ပျိုး
myant	myan	myann	phyawt	phyaw	phyaww	pyoht	pyo	pyoh

Practice reading these words that contain ya. Trace the gray letters then practice writing them freehand. You can challenge yourself further by writing the whole word.

1. a <u>pyar</u>   blue

    အပြာ

2. a <u>myarr</u> <u>kyee</u>   a lot

    အများကြီး

3. <u>myoht</u> taw   capital city

    မြို့တော်

4. a <u>cho</u>   sweet

    အချို

5. <u>myay</u> peh   peanut

    မြေပဲ

6. <u>phyaw</u> yi   juice

    ဖျော်ရည်

7. <u>kyann</u> mar tae   healthy

    ကျန်းမာတယ်

8. <u>Pyaw</u> larr?   Are you happy?

    ပျော်လား။

9. <u>Myarr</u> <u>myarr</u> sarr par.   Eat a lot.

    များများစားပါ။

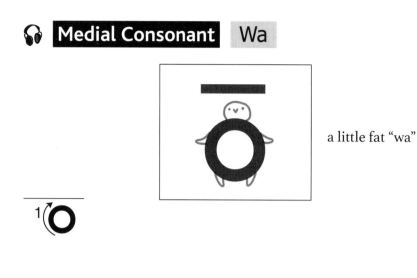

🎧 Medial Consonant　Wa

a little fat "wa"

1 ⟳O

— wa
o

Above is the medial consonant addition for wa. It can be added to consonants alone or consonants and vowels together, to form different tones. To attach this medial consonant, the above addition is written below the consonant on the right side.

Practice tracing the example vowel and consonant combinations.

ကွ	ကွာ	ကွား	ခွိတ်	ခွိ	ခွီး	ဆွေ့	ဆွေ	ဆွေး
kwa	kwar	kwarr	khweet	khwi	khwee	swayt	sway	swayy

တွဲ့	တွယ်	တွဲ	နွေ့	နွေ	နွေး	ပွဲ့	ပွယ်	ပွဲ
twaet	twae	tweh	nwayt	nway	nwayy	pwaet	pwae	pweh

ကျွ	ကျွာ	ကျွား	ကျွေ့	ကျွေ	ကျွေး	ချွဲ့	ချွယ်	ချွဲ
kywa	kywar	kywarr	kywayt	kyway	kywayy	chwaet	chwae	chweh

ကျွေ့	ကျွေ	ကျွေး	တွေ့	တွေ	တွေး	ရွဲ့	ရွယ်	ရွဲ
gywayt	gyway	gywayy	twayt	tway	twayy	ywaet	ywae	yweh

Practice reading these words that contain wa. Trace the gray letters then practice writing them freehand. You can challenge yourself further by writing the whole word.

1. <u>ywar</u>   village

ရွာ

2. sarr <u>pweh</u>   table

စားပွဲ

3. a <u>bwarr</u>   grandmother

အဘွား

4. <u>nway</u> yar thi   summer

နွေရာသီ

5. <u>pweh</u> taw   festival

ပွဲတော်

6. <u>lwae</u> tae   easy

လွယ်တယ်

7. tha <u>khwarr</u> thee   cucumber

သခွါးသီး

8. <u>ngway</u> sweh kyoh   silver necklace

ငွေဆွဲကြိုး

9. <u>nwarr</u> noht   cow's milk

နွားနို့

🎧 Revision: Reading Practice

You should now be able to read the words below. Cover the right-hand column of text so you can only see the Burmese script on the left-hand side of the page. Try reading each Burmese word aloud and then uncover the column on the right to check. Keep practicing until you can read them all. For an extra challenge see if you can remember the English meaning before checking.

Burmese	Romanization (English)
သော့	thawt (key)
ကော်ဇော	kaw zaww (carpet)
မောတယ်	maww tae (tired)
ဒေါသ	daww tha (anger)
အဒေါ်	a daw (aunt)
စောစော	saww saww (early)
အပေါ်	a paw (on)
တယော	ta yaww (violin)
တောသူ	taww thu (country bumpkin girl)
လမ်း	lann (street)
အခန်း	a khann (room)
အတန်း	a tann (class)
ပန်းသီး	pann thee (apple)
ငန်တယ်	ngan tae (salty)
နံရံ	nan yan (wall)
အရမ်း	a yann (very)
ခရမ်းသီး	kha yann thee (eggplant)
အခမ်းအနား	a khann a narr (ceremony)
ခို	kho (pigeon)
အဘိုး	a boh (grandfather)
ပုဆိုး	poot soh (male longyi [traditional skirt])
မီးဖို	mee pho (stove)
နို့ဆီ	noht si (condensed milk)

အညို	a nyo (brown)
သူခိုး	thu khoh (thief)
ဒီလိုပါပဲ	di lo par peh (so-so)
စာပို့သမား	sar poht tha marr (postman)
အပြာ	a pyar (blue)
အများကြီး	a myarr kyee (a lot)
မြို့တော်	myoht taw (capital city)
အချို	a cho (sweet)
မြေပဲ	myay peh (peanut)
ဖျော်ရည်	phyaw yi (juice)
ကျန်းမာတယ်	kyann mar tae (healthy)
ပျော်လား။	Pyaw larr? (Are you happy?)
မြန်မြန်စားပါ။	Myan myan sarr par. (Please eat quickly.)
ရွာ	ywar (village)
စားပွဲ	sarr pweh (table)
အဘွား	a bwarr (grandmother)
နွေရာသီ	nway yar thi (summer)
ပွဲတော်	pweh taw (festival)
လွယ်တယ်	lwae tae (easy)
သခွားသီး	tha khwarr thee (cucumber)
ငွေဆွဲကြိုး	ngway sweh kyoh (silver necklace)
နွားနို့	nwarr noht (milk)

Aspirated Sound   Ha

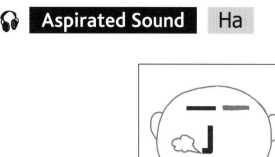

breathe through your nose to make an aspirated sound

J̲   ha

If a sound is aspirated, it is accompanied by a small puff of air when spoken, like the "p" in "puff." The nasal aspiration of some sounds in Burmese can be achieved by consciously breathing out through the nose at the same time as speaking the sound.

Above is the addition to make consonants aspirated. It can be added to consonants alone or consonants and vowels together, to form different tones. Note that if the consonant ရ ya is joined by the aspirated addition ̲ ha, it becomes ှ sha (not yha).

The above addition is written below the consonant.

Practice tracing the example vowel and consonant combinations.

င	ငာ	ငား	မ	မာ	မား	ရ	ရာ	ရား
ngha	nghar	ngharr	mha	mhar	mharr	sha	shar	sharr

ရို့	ရို	ရိုး	လေ့	လေ	လေး	ရှိ	ရှိ	ရှီ
shoht	sho	shoh	hlayt	hlay	hlayy	sheet	shi	shee

မူ	မူ	မူး	လှန့်	လှန်	လှန်း	နို့	နို	နိုး
mhoot	mhu	mhoo	hlant	hlan	hlann	nhoht	nho	nhoh

မှော့	မှော်	မှော	ငဲ့	ငယ်	ငဲ	မို့	မို	မိုး
mhawt	mhaw	mhaww	nghaet	nghae	ngheh	mhoht	mho	mhoh

🎧 **Reading and Writing Practice** | Ha

Practice reading these words that contain ha. Trace the gray letters then practice writing them freehand. You can challenge yourself further by writing the whole word.

1. <u>hla</u> tae   beautiful

   လှတယ်

2. <u>mho</u>   mushroom

   မှို

3. <u>hlay</u>   boat

   လှေ

4. a <u>shayt</u>   in front

   အရှေ့

5. Bar <u>mhar</u> ma leh?   What would you like to order?

   ဘာမှာမလဲ။

6. a <u>hlu</u>   donation ceremony (at a Buddhist monastery)

   အလှူ။

7. <u>shu</u> sayy   inhaler

   ရှူဆေး

8. <u>Mhan</u> larr?   Is that right?

   မှန်လား။

9. <u>Mharr</u> nay tae.   That's wrong.

   မှားနေတယ်။

🎧 **Vowel Formation**   Et

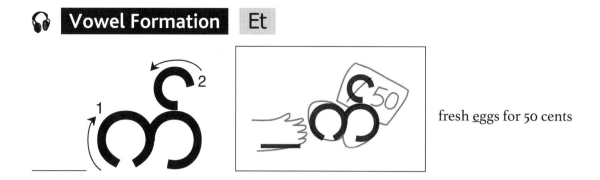

fresh <u>e</u>ggs for 50 cents

_က်   et as in egg (stopped tone)

Et has only one tone, which is high and very short. To form this vowel, the above addition is written to the right of the consonant.

Practice tracing the example vowel and consonant combinations.

ကက်	ခက်	စက်	ဆက်	ဇက်	ညက်	တက်	ထက်
ket	khet	set	set	zet	nyet	tet	htet

နက်	ပက်	ဖက်	ဘက်	မက်	ယက်	ရက်	လက်
net	pet	phet	bet	met	yet	yet	let

ဝက်	သက်	ဟက်	အက်	ကြက်	ချက်	ပျက်	မျက်
wet	thet	het	et	kyet	chet	pyet	myet

🎧 **Reading and Writing Practice**   Et

Trace the gray letters, then practice writing the words freehand.

1. <u>wet</u> pig

ဝက် ....

2. <u>wet</u> tharr   pork

ဝက်သား ....

3. kyet tharr   chicken

ကြက်သား ....

4. kyet oot   chicken egg

ကြက်ဥ ....

5. <u>let</u> phet   tea leaf

လက်ဖက် ....

6. tha <u>yet</u> thee   mango

သရက်သီး ....

7. sar <u>myet</u> nhar   page

စာမျက်နှာ ....

8. <u>ket set</u>   cassette

ကက်ဆက် ....

🎧 Vowel Formation   At

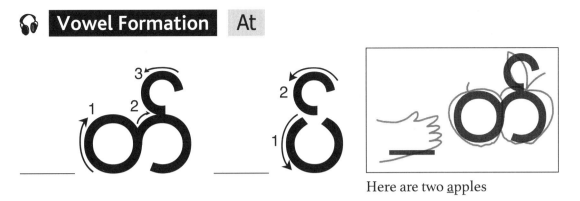

Here are two <u>a</u>pples

__တ်   or   __ိ်   a as in apple (stopped tone)

At has only one tone, which is high and very short. To form this vowel, the above additions are written to the right of the consonant. Any consonant can be joined by either of the above versions of at.

Practice tracing the example vowel and consonant combinations.

ကတ်	ခတ်	ငတ်	ဆတ်	တတ်	နတ်	ပတ်	ဖတ်
kat	khat	ngat	sat	tat	nat	pat	phat

ဘတ်	မတ်	ရပ်	သပ်	အပ်	ကြပ်	ချပ်	ပြတ်
bat	mat	yat	that	at	kyat	chat	pyat

ဖျတ်	မြတ်	ကြတ်	ကျပ်
phyat	myat	kyat	kyat

🎧 Reading and Writing Practice   At

Trace the gray letters, then practice writing the words freehand.

1. a <u>pat</u>   week

အ ပတ်   ....

2. <u>sat</u> tae   spicy

စပ်တယ် ....

3. sar <u>phat</u> tae   to read

စာဖတ်တယ် ....

4. <u>nat</u> tha mee   angel

နတ်သမီး ....

5. myan mar <u>kyat</u>   Myanmar currency

မြန်မာကျပ် ....

7. karr <u>kyat</u> tae   traffic jam

ကားတယ် ....

....

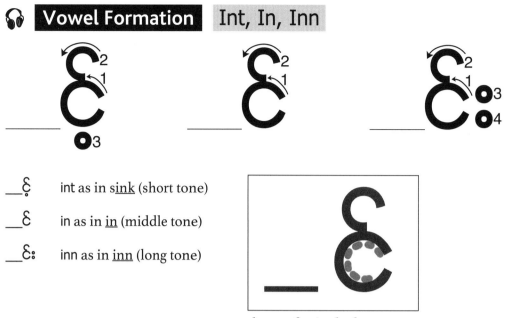

___ ${\tiny o}$ C   int as in s<u>ink</u> (short tone)

___ C   in as in <u>in</u> (middle tone)

___ C: inn as in <u>inn</u> (long tone)

the top fits <u>in</u> the bottom

To form this vowel, the above additions are written to the right of the consonant.

*Note that when the aspirated sound ha is joined to the medial consonant wa, ha attaches horizontally to the left side of wa. This can be seen in the combinations nhwint, nhwin, nhwinn on the bottom line of the chart below. It can also be seen in some combinations on page 75 and page 77.

Practice tracing the example vowel and consonant combinations.

ကင့်	ကင်	ကင်း	cင့်	cင်	cင်း	ညင့်	ညင်	ညင်း
kint	kin	kinn	ngint	ngin	nginn	nyint	nyin	nyinn

တင့်	တင်	တင်း	ထင့်	ထင်	ထင်း	နင့်	နင်	နင်း
tint	tin	tinn	htint	htin	htinn	nint	nin	ninn

ျင့်	ျင်	ျင်း	ွင့်	ွင်	ွင်း	မြင့်	မြင်	မြင်း
pyint	pyin	pyinn	phwint	phwin	phwinn	myint	myin	myinn

နွင့်	နွင်	နွင်း	နှင့်	နှင်	နှင်း	မှင့်	မှင်	မှင်း
nhwint	nhwin	nhwinn	nhint	nhin	nhinn	mhint	mhin	mhinn

🎧 Reading and Writing Practice — Int, In, Inn

Practice reading these words that contain int, in or inn. Trace the gray letters then practice writing them freehand. You can challenge yourself further by writing the whole word.

1. hta <u>minn</u>   cooked rice

   ထမင်း ....

2. ngarr <u>kin</u>   grilled fish

   ငါးကင် ....

3. <u>htin</u> tae   to think

   ထင်တယ် ....

4. kyet <u>kin</u>   roast chicken

   ကင် ....

5. <u>Win</u> lar par.   Please come in.

   ဝင်လာပါ။ ....

6. <u>kyin</u> nar tae   kind

   နာတယ် ....

7. <u>phwint</u> tae   to open, turn on

   ဖွင့်တယ် ....

8. <u>pyinn</u> tae   bored, lazy

   ပျင်းတယ် ....

 **Vowel Formation** It

"There's a mouse in the salon—
<u>IT</u>'S IN MY HAIR!"

__**စ်**   it as in sit (stopped tone)

It has only one tone, which is high and very short. To form this vowel, the above addition is written to the right of the consonant.

Practice tracing the example vowel and consonant combinations.

ကစ်	ညစ်	တစ်	နစ်	ရစ်	လစ်	သစ်	ဟစ်	အစ်
kit	nyit	tit	nit	yit	lit	thit	hit	it

ချစ်	ဂျစ်	ပျစ်	ဖြစ်	မြစ်	ခြစ်	မျှစ်	ရှစ်	နှစ်
chit	gyit	pyit	phyit	myit	chit	mhyit	shit	nhit

 Reading and Writing Practice It

Trace the gray letters, then practice writing the words freehand.

1. <u>tit</u>   one

    တစ် ....

2. saet <u>nhit</u>   twelve

   ဆယ့်နစ် ....

3. ma <u>nhit</u> ka   last year

   မနစ်က ....

4. <u>nyit</u> pat tae   dirty

   ညစ်ပတ်တယ် ....

5. <u>shit</u> sae   eighty

    ရှစ်ဆယ် ....

6. Ay yar wa ti <u>myit</u>   Ayeyarwaddy river

   ဧရာဝတီမြစ် ....

7. a <u>thit</u>   new

   အသစ် ....

8. Bar <u>phyit</u> loht leh?   Why?

   ဘာဖြစ်လို့လဲ။ ....

   ....

🎧 Revision: Reading Practice

You should now be able to read the words below. Cover the right-hand column of text so you can only see the Burmese script on the left-hand side of the page. Try reading each Burmese word aloud and then uncover the column on the right to check. Keep practicing until you can read them all. For an extra challenge see if you can remember the English meaning before checking.

လှတယ်	hla tae (beautiful)
မှို	mho (mushroom)
အရှေ့	a shayt (in front)
ဘာမှာမလဲ။	Bar mhar ma leh? (What would you like to order?)
အလှူ	a hlu (donation ceremony at a Buddhist monastery)
ရှူဆေး	shu sayy (inhaler)
မှန်လား။	Mhan larr? (Is that right?)
မှားနေတယ်။	Mharr nay tae. (That's wrong.)
ဝက်	wet (pig)
ဝက်သား	wet tharr (pork)
ကြက်သား	kyet tharr (chicken)
ကြက်ဥ	kyet oot (chicken egg)
လက်ဖက်	let phet (tea leaf)
သရက်သီး	tha yet thee (mango)
စာမျက်နှာ	sar myet nhar (page)
ကက်ဆက်	ket set (cassette)
ခက်တယ်	khet tae (difficult)
အပတ်	a pat (week)
စပ်တယ်	sat tae (spicy)
နတ်သမီး	nat tha mee (angel)
စာဖတ်တယ်	sar phat tae (to read)
မတ်တပ်ရပ်ပါ။	Mat tat yat par. (Please stand up.)
မြန်မာကျပ်	myan mar kyat (Myanmar currency)

ကားကြပ်တယ်	karr kyat tae (traffic jam)
လူသတ်သမား	lu that tha marr (murderer)
သွက်လက်ဖျတ်လတ်တယ်	thwet let phyat lat tae (strong and active)
ထမင်း	hta minn (cooked rice)
ငါးကင်	ngarr kin (grilled fish)
ထင်တယ်	htin tae (to think)
ကြက်ကင်	kyet kin (roast chicken)
ဝင်လာပါ။	Win lar par. (Please come in.)
ကြင်နာတယ်	kyin nar tae (kind)
ဖွင့်တယ်	phwint tae (to open, turn on)
ပျင်းတယ်	pyinn tae (bored, lazy)
သူနဲ့ခင်လား။	Thu naet khin larr? (Are you close to him?)
တစ်	tit (one)
ဆယ့်နှစ်	saet nhit (twelve)
မနှစ်က	ma nhit ka (last year)
ညစ်ပတ်တယ်	nyit pat tae (dirty)
ရှစ်ဆယ်	shit sae (eighty)
ဧရာဝတီမြစ်	Ay yar wa ti myit (Ayeyarwaddy river)
အသစ်	a thit (new)
ဘာဖြစ်လို့လဲ။	Bar phyit loht leh? (Why?)
ဘာဖြစ်လို့လဲဆိုတော့	bar phyit loht leh so tawt (because)

🎧 Vowel Formation 'Ownt, 'Own, 'Ownn

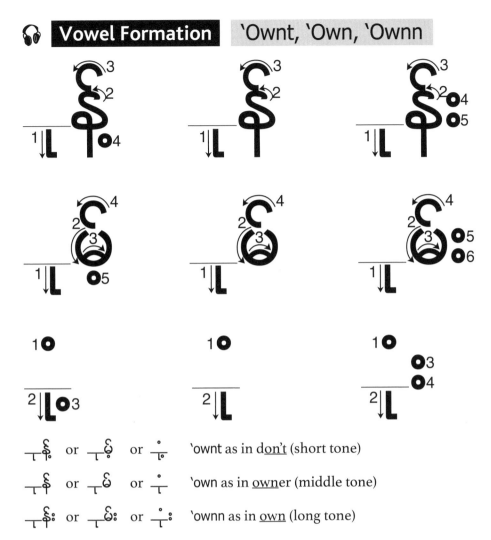

—┬ᷥ᷄ or —┬ᷥ᷄ or ᷝ 'ownt as in <u>don't</u> (short tone)

—┬ᷥ or —┬ᷥ or ᷝ 'own as in <u>owner</u> (middle tone)

—┬ᷥ: or —┬ᷥ: or ᷝ: 'ownn as in <u>own</u> (long tone)

To form this vowel, use the additions as shown above. Any consonant can be joined by any of the above versions of 'ownt, 'own or 'ownn.

Practice tracing the example vowel and consonant combinations.

ကုန့်	ကုန်	ကုန်း	တုန့်	တုန်	တုန်း	မုန့်	မုန်	မုန်း
k'ownt	k'own	k'ownn	t'ownt	t'own	t'ownn	m'ownt	m'own	m'ownn

စုမ့်	စုမ်	စုမ်း	ရုမ့်	ရုမ်	ရုမ်း	လုမ့်	လုမ်	လုမ်း
s'ownt	s'own	s'ownn	y'ownt	y'own	y'ownn	l'ownt	l'own	l'ownn

ဆုံ့	ဆုံ	ဆုံး	န့	န	န:	ဖုံ့	ဖုံ	ဖုံး
s'ownt	s'own	s'ownn	n'ownt	n'own	n'ownn	ph'ownt	ph'own	ph'ownn

Vowels **61**

Practice reading these words that contain 'ownt, 'own, or 'ownn vowels. Trace the gray letters then practice writing them freehand. You can challenge yourself further by writing the whole word.

1. kh'own chair

   ခုံ

2. arr l'ownn all

   အားလုံး

3. a k'own all

   အကုန်

4. yay kheh m'ownt ice cream

   ရေခဲမုန့်

5. y'own tae believe, trust

   ယုံတယ်

6. dat p'own photo

   ဓာတ်ပုံ

7. dat p'own sa yar photographer

   ဓာတ်ပုံဆရာ

8. tae li ph'ownn telephone

   တယ်လီဖုန်း

9. m'ownn tae hate

   မုန်းတယ်

🎧 **Vowel Formation** Out

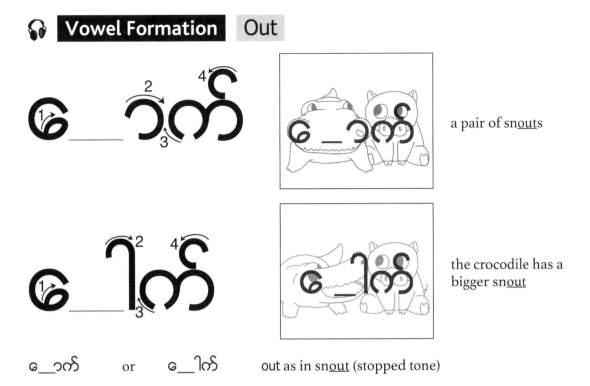

a pair of sn<u>out</u>s

the crocodile has a bigger sn<u>out</u>

ေ___ာက်   or   ေ__ိက်   out as in sn<u>out</u> (stopped tone)

Out has only one tone, which is high and very short.

Above is the standard vowel addition for out. The addition in the second line are used with the consonants အ, ဂ, င, ဒ, ပ and ဝ to avoid confusion.

Practice tracing the example vowel and consonant combinations.

ကောက်	ခေါက်	ဂေါက်	ငေါက်	ဆောက်	တောက်
kout	khout	gout	ngout	sout	tout

ထောက်	ဒေါက်	နောက်	ပေါက်	ဖောက်	ဘောက်
htout	dout	nout	pout	phout	bout

မောက်	ယောက်	ရောက်	လောက်	သောက်	ဟောက်
mout	yout	yout	lout	thout	hout

အောက်	ကျောက်	ခြောက်	မျောက်	ရှောက်	
out	kyout	chout	myout	shout	

Reading and Writing Practice — Out

Practice reading these words that contain the out vowel. Trace the gray letters then practice writing them freehand. You can challenge yourself further by writing the whole word.

1. a nout behind

   အနောက်

2. out mhar under, below

   အောက်မှာ

3. Bar thout ma leh? What would you like to drink?

   ဘာသောက်မလဲ။

4. kyout tae scared, frightened

   ကြောက်တယ်

5. kyout t'ownn stone

   ကျောက်တုံး

6. Bae lout leh? How much?

   ဘယ်လောက်လဲ။

7. Bae nhit khout leh? How many times?

   ဘယ်နှစ်ခေါက်လဲ။

8. khout sweh kyaw fried noodles

   ခေါက်ဆွဲကြော်

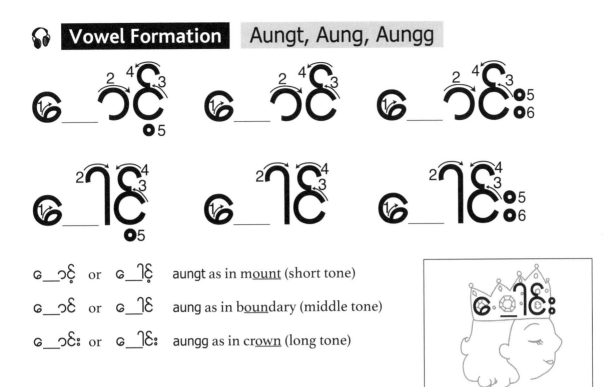

ေ__ာင့် or ေ__ိုင့်   aungt as in m<u>oun</u>t (short tone)

ေ__ာင် or ေ__ိုင်   aung as in b<u>oun</u>dary (middle tone)

ေ__ာင်း or ေ__ိုင်း   aungg as in cr<u>own</u> (long tone)

the queen's cr<u>own</u> is tall

The additions in the second line are used with the consonants ခ, ဂ, င, ဒ, ပ and ဝ to avoid confusion.

Practice tracing the example vowel and consonant combinations.

ကောင့်	ကောင်	ကောင်း	စောင့်	စောင်	စောင်း	ထောင့်
kaungt	kaung	kaungg	saungt	saung	saungg	htaungt

ထောင်	ထောင်း	နောင့်	နောင်	နောင်း	ရောင့်	ရောင်
htaung	htaungg	naungt	naung	naungg	yaungt	yaung

ရောင်း	ခေါင့်	ခေါင်	ခေါင်း	ဒေါင့်	ဒေါင်	ဒေါင်း
yaungg	khaungt	khaung	khaungg	daungt	daung	daungg

ကျောင့်	ကျောင်	ကျောင်း	မြောင့်	မြောင်	မြောင်း
kyaungt	kyaung	kyaungg	myaungt	myaung	myaungg

 **Reading and Writing Practice**   Aungt, Aung, Aungg

Practice reading these words that contain aungt, aung, or aungg vowels. Trace the gray letters then practice writing them freehand. You can challenge yourself further by writing the whole word.

1. kyaung   cat

    ကြောင်

2. kyaungg   school

   ကျောင်း

3. kyaungg tharr   student

   ကျောင်းသား

4. a haungg   old, not new

   အဟောင်း

5. maung layy   little brother

   မောင်လေး

6. khaungg moo tae   dizzy

    ခေါင်းမူးတယ်

7. naung ta ya tae   to regret

   နောင်တရတယ်

8. taung tet thwarr tae   to go hiking

    တောင်တက်သွားတယ်

9. soot soot paungg   total

   စုစုပေါင်း

🎧 Vowel Formation   Ote

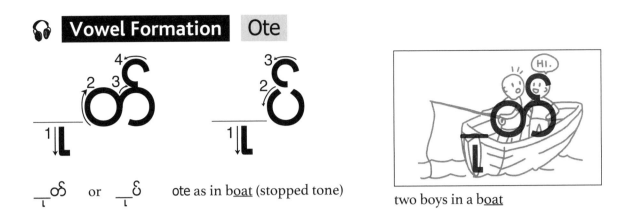

အုတ်   or   အို်   ote as in b<u>oat</u> (stopped tone)

two boys in a b<u>oat</u>

To form this vowel, use the additions as shown above. Any consonant can be joined by either of the above versions of ote.

Practice tracing the example vowel and consonant combinations.

ကုတ်	ခုတ်	ဆုတ်	တုတ်	နုတ်	ဖုတ်	ယုတ်	သုတ်	ဟုတ်
kote	khote	sote	tote	note	phote	yote	thote	hote

ကျုပ်	ခြုပ်	စုပ်	ပြုတ်	ဖြုတ်	မြုပ်	လုပ်	လှုပ်	ရှုပ်	အုပ်
kyote	chote	sote	pyote	phyote	mhyote	lote	hlote	shote	ote

✍ Reading and Writing Practice   Ote

Trace the gray letters, then practice writing the words freehand.

1. a <u>lote</u>   work

    အလုပ် ....

2 . a <u>thote</u>   salad

    အသုပ် ....

3. sar <u>ote</u>   book

    စာအုပ် ....

4. ta <u>yote</u> za garr   Chinese language

    တရုတ်စကား ....

5. nga <u>yote</u> thee   chili

    ငရုတ်သီး ....

6. let phet <u>thote</u>   tea leaf salad

    လက်ဖက်သုပ် ....

7. <u>hote</u> tae   yes; that's true

    ဟုတ်တယ် ....

8. a <u>lote</u> myarr tae   busy

    အလုပ်များတယ် ....

Vowel Formation — Ate

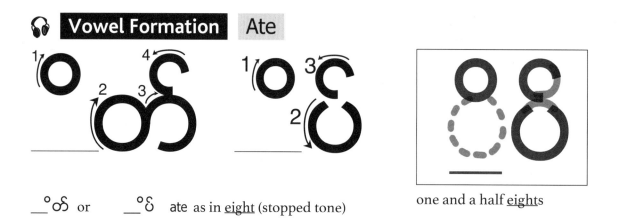

___°တ် or ___°ိ   ate as in <u>eight</u> (stopped tone)

one and a half <u>eights</u>

To form this vowel, use the additions as shown above. Any consonant can be joined by either of the above versions of ate.

Practice tracing the example vowel and consonant combinations.

ကိတ်	စိတ်	ဆိတ်	တိတ်	ထိပ်	ပိတ်	ဖိတ်	ဘိတ်	မိတ်
kate	sate	sate	tate	htate	pate	phate	bate	mate

လိပ်	အိတ်	ကြိတ်	ချိတ်	မြိတ်	ရှိတ်	မှိတ်	အိပ်	နှိပ်	ရိတ်
late	ate	kyate	chate	myate	shate	mhate	ate	nhate	yate

Reading and Writing Practice — Ate

Trace the gray letters, then practice writing the words freehand.

1. sar <u>ate</u>   envelope
   စာအိတ်

2. <u>late</u> sar   address
   လိပ်စာ

3. lay <u>sate</u>   airport
   လေဆိပ်

4. <u>sate</u> soh tae   angry
   စိတ်ဆိုးတယ်

5. <u>ate</u> chin tae   sleepy
   အိပ်ချင်တယ်

6. Tan kharr <u>pate</u> par.   Please close the door.
   တံခါးပိတ်ပါ။

7. kate m'ownt   cake
   ကိတ်မုန့်

8. mwayy nayt <u>phate</u> sar   birthday invitation
   မွေးနေ့ဖိတ်စာ

🎧 Revision: Reading Practice

You should now be able to read the words below. Cover the right-hand column of text so you can only see the Burmese script on the left-hand side of the page. Try reading each Burmese word aloud and then uncover the column on the right to check. Keep practicing until you can read them all. For an extra challenge see if you can remember the English meaning before checking.

ခုံ	kh'own (chair)
အားလုံး	arr l'ownn (all)
အကုန်	a k'own (all)
ရေခဲမုန့်	yay kheh m'ownt (ice cream)
ယုံတယ်	y'own tae (to believe, to trust)
ဓာတ်ပုံ	dat p'own (photo)
ဓာတ်ပုံဆရာ	dat p'own sa yar (photographer)
တယ်လီဖုန်း	tae li ph'ownn (telephone)
မုန်းတယ်	m'ownn tae (hate)
အနောက်	a nout (behind)
အောက်မှာ	out mhar (under, below)
ဘာသောက်မလဲ။	Bar thout ma leh? (What would you like to drink?)
ကြောက်တယ်	kyout tae (scared, frightened)
ကျောက်တုံး	kyout t'ownn (stone)
ဘယ်လောက်လဲ။	Bae lout leh? (How much?)
ဘယ်နှစ်ခေါက်လဲ။	Bae nhit khout leh? (How many times?)
ခေါက်ဆွဲကြော်	khout sweh kyaw (fried noodles)
သောက်တယ်	thout tae (to drink)
ကြောင်	kyaung (cat)
ကျောင်း	kyaungg (school)
ကျောင်းသား	kyaungg tharr (student)
အဟောင်း	a haungg (old, not new)
မောင်လေး	maung layy (little brother)

ခေါင်းမူးတယ်	khaungg moo tae (dizzy)
နောင်တရတယ်	naung ta ya tae (to regret)
တောင်တက်သွားတယ်	taung tet thwarr tae (to go hiking)
စုစုပေါင်း	soot soot paungg (total)
အလုပ်	a lote (work)
တရုတ်စကား	ta yote za garr (Chinese language)
စာအုပ်	sar ote (book)
အသုပ်	a thote (salad)
ငရုတ်သီး	nga yote thee (chili)
လက်ဖက်သုပ်	let phet thote (tea leaf salad)
အလုပ်များတယ်	a lote myarr tae (busy)
ဟုတ်တယ်	hote tae (yes; that's true)
ဘယ်မှာအလုပ်လုပ်လဲ။	Bae mhar a lote lote leh? (Where do you work?)
စာအိတ်	sar ate (envelope)
လိပ်စာ	late sar (address)
စိတ်ဆိုးတယ်	sate soh tae (angry)
လေဆိပ်	lay sate (airport)
အိပ်ချင်တယ်	ate chin tae (sleepy)
မွေးနေ့ဖိတ်စာ	mwayy nayt phate sar (birthday invitation)
ကိတ်မုန့်	kate m'ownt (cake)
တံခါးပိတ်ပါ။	Tan kharr pate par. (Please close the door.)
စိတ်ဝင်စားစရာကောင်းတယ်	sate win sarr sa yar kaungg tae (interesting)

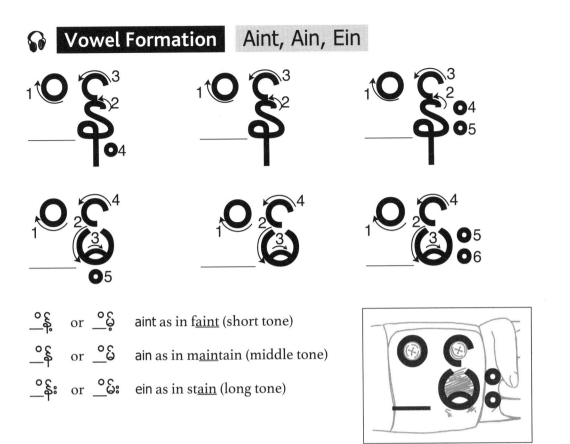

___ န့ ် or ___ မ့ ် aint as in f<u>aint</u> (short tone)

___ န ် or ___ မ ် ain as in m<u>ain</u>tain (middle tone)

___ န ်း or ___ မ ်း ein as in st<u>ain</u> (long tone)

my sleeve has a st<u>ain</u>!

To form this vowel, use the additions as shown above. Any consonant can be joined by any of the above versions of aint, ain, ein.

Practice tracing the example vowel and consonant combinations.

ကိန့်	ကိန်	ကိန်း	စိန့်	စိန်	စိန်း	ထိန့်	ထိန်	ထိန်း
kaint	kain	kein	saint	sain	sein	htaint	htain	htein

ပိန့်	ပိန်	ပိန်း	ဆိမ့်	ဆိမ်	ဆိမ်း	ညိမ့်	ညိမ်	ညိမ်း
paint	pain	pein	saint	sain	sein	nyaint	nyain	nyein

နိမ့်	နိမ်	နိမ်း	ကျိန့်	ကျိန်	ကျိန်း	ခြိမ့်	ခြိမ်	ခြိမ်း
naint	nain	nein	kyaint	kyain	kyein	chaint	chain	chein

Reading and Writing Practice — Aint, Ain, Ein

Practice reading these words that contain aint, ain, or ein vowels. Trace the gray letters then practice writing them freehand. You can challenge yourself further by writing the whole word.

1. sain diamond

   စိန်

2. hta main female longyi (traditional skirt)

   ထမိန်

3. lu lain liar

   လူလိမ်

4. pain tae thin, not fat

   ပိန်တယ်

5. bein phyu opium

   ဘိန်းဖြူ

6. sain sweh kyoh diamond necklace

   စိန်ဆွဲကြိုး

7. a sein yaung green

   အစိမ်းရောင်

8. tain htu tae cloudy

   တိမ်ထူတယ်

9. Eain ka bae mhar leh? Where's your house?

   အိမ်ကဘယ်မှာလဲ။

🎧 Vowel Formation Ite

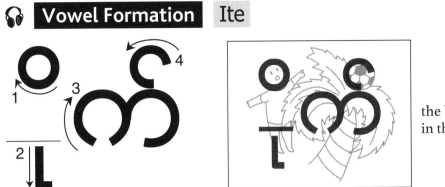

the ball <u>might</u> be stuck in that tree

  ite as in m<u>ight</u> (stopped tone)

Ite has only one tone, which is high and very short. To form this vowel, use the additon as shown above.

Practice tracing the example vowel and consonant combinations.

ကိုက်	ငိုက်	ဆိုက်	တိုက်	နိုက်	ပိုက်	ဗိုက်	မိုက်
kite	ngite	site	tite	nite	pite	bite	mite

ရိုက်	လိုက်	ကြိုက်	ချိုက်	ပြိုက်	ဗျိုက်	မြိုက်	ရှိုက်
yite	lite	kyite	chite	pyite	byite	myite	shite

လှိုက်	ဝိုက်	အိုက်
hlite	white	eite

🎧 Reading and Writing Practice Ite

Trace the gray letters, then practice writing the words freehand.

1. site karr   trishaw
   ဆိုက်ကား ....

2. kyite tae   to like
   ကြိုက်တယ် ....

3. bite sar tae   hungry
   ဗိုက်ဆာတယ် ....

4. Lite ma larr?   Will you come with me?
   လိုက်မလား။ ....

5. eite tae   to feel hot
   အိုက်တယ် ....

6. bite aungt tae   stomachache
   ဗိုက်အောင့်တယ် ....

🎧 Vowel Formation   Ainq, Ai, Aii

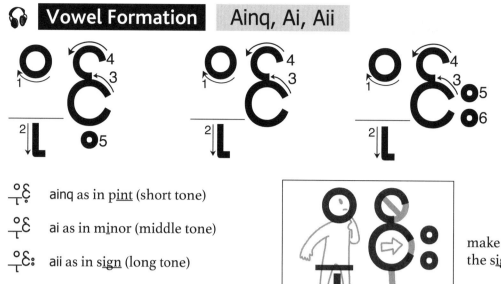

ainq as in p<u>i</u>nt (short tone)

ai as in m<u>i</u>nor (middle tone)

aii as in s<u>ig</u>n (long tone)

make sure to read the si<u>gn</u>s

To form this vowel, use the additions as shown above.
Practice tracing the example vowel and consonant combinations.

kainq	kai	kaii	khainq	khai	khaii	sainq	sai	saii
htainq	htai	htaii	nainq	nai	naii	mainq	mai	maii
kyainq	kyai	kyaii	pyainq	pyai	pyaii	hlainq	hlai	hlaii

🎧 Reading and Writing Practice   Ainq, Ai, Aii

Trace the gray letters, then practice writing the words freehand.

1. <u>s</u>ai   <u>s</u>hop

....

2. pai shin   owner

....

3. thaii nai ngan   Thailand

....

4. sa pyit wai   Burmese grape wine

....

5. yaii tae   rude

....

6. ya khai pyi nae   Rakhine State

....

74 PART TWO

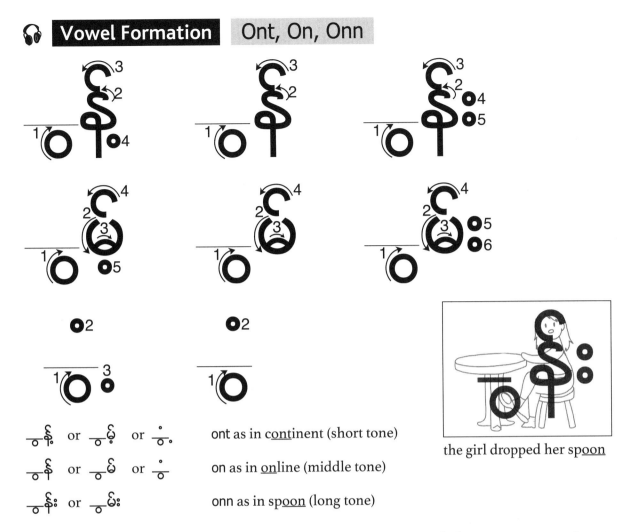

the girl dropped her sp<u>oo</u>n

ont as in c<u>onti</u>nent (short tone)

on as in <u>on</u>line (middle tone)

onn as in sp<u>oo</u>n (long tone)

Above are the standard vowel additions for ont, on, onn. In some words they are pronounced want, wan, wann. To form this vowel, use the additions as shown above. Any consonant can be joined by any of the above versions of ont, on, onn.

Practice tracing the example vowel and consonant combinations.

ကွန့်	ကွန်	ကွန်း	ခွန့်	ခွန်	ခွန်း	စွန့်	စွန်	စွန်း
kont	kon	konn	khont	khon	khonn	sont	son	sonn

တွန့်	တွန်	တွန်း	မွန့်	မွန်	မွန်း	လွမ့်	လွမ်	လွမ်း
tont	ton	tonn	mont	mon	monn	lwant	lwan	lwann

ကွမ့်	ကွမ်	ကွမ်း	ကျွန့်	ကျွန်	ကျွန်း	ရွန့်	ရွန်	ရွန်း
kont	kon	konn	kyont	kyon	kyonn	shont	shon	shonn

Reading and Writing Practice Ont, On, Onn

Practice reading these words that contain ont, on, or onn vowels. Trace the gray letters then practice writing them freehand. You can challenge yourself further by writing the whole word.

.

1. konn   betel nut

ကွမ်း

2. lwann tae   to miss

လွမ်းတယ်

3. mon pyi nae   Mon State

မွန်ပြည်နယ်

4. kon yet   network

ကွန်ရက်

5. Zonn sheet larr?   Do you have a spoon?

ဇွန်းရှိလား။

6. lann nhyon   guide, directory

လမ်းညွှန်

7. Honn ma tee par naet.   Please don't use your horn.

ဟွန်းမတီးပါနဲ့။

8. khon arr   strength

ခွန်အား

9. yonn   lacquer

ယွန်း

🎧 **Vowel Formation** Ut

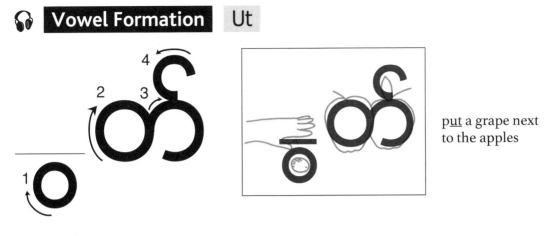

put a grape next
to the apples

◌ွတ် ut as in put (stopped tone)

Ut has only one tone, which is high and very short. To form this vowel, use the above addition.

Practice tracing the example vowel and consonant combinations.

ကွတ်	ဆွတ်	ညွတ်	တွတ်	ပွတ်	ဖွတ်	မွတ်	ရွတ်	လွတ်	သွတ်
kut	sut	nyut	tut	put	phut	mut	yut	lut	thut

ကျွတ်	ချွတ်	ပြွတ်	လွွတ်	ရွှတ်	နွှတ်	မွှတ်	ညွှတ်	ကြွတ်
kyut	chut	pyut	hlut	shut	nhut	mhut	nyhut	kyut

🎧 **Reading and Writing Practice** Ut

Trace the gray letters, then practice writing the words freehand.

1. put tae   to rub

   ပွတ်တယ်

2. but pheet nat   boots

   ဘွတ်ဖိနပ်

3. mut sa lin   Muslim

   မွတ်ဆလင်

4. yay mwayy sut tae   to put on perfume

   ရေမွှေးဆွတ်တယ်

5. a htut a myat   holy

   အထွတ်အမြတ်

6. tar yar kyut   tire tube

   တာယာကျွတ်

7. chut tae   to take off

   ချွတ်တယ်

8. khwint hlut tae   to forgive

   ခွင့်လွတ်တယ်

You should now be able to read the words below. Cover the right-hand column of text so you can only see the Burmese script on the left-hand side of the page. Try reading each Burmese word aloud and then uncover the column on the right to check. Keep practicing until you can read them all. For an extra challenge see if you can remember the English meaning before checking.

စိန်	sain (diamond)
ထဘိန်	hta main (female longyi [traditional skirt])
လူလိမ်	lu lain (liar)
ပိန်တယ်	pain tae (thin, not fat)
ဘိန်းဖြူ	bein phyu (opium)
စိန်ဆွဲကြိုး	sain sweh kyoh (diamond necklace)
အစိမ်းရောင်	a sein yaung (green)
တိမ်ထူတယ်	tain htu tae (cloudy)
အိမ်ကဘယ်မှာလဲ။	Eain ka bae mhar leh? (Where's your house?)
ဆိုက်ကား	site karr (trishaw)
ကြိုက်တယ်	kyite tae (to like)
ဗိုက်ဆာတယ်	bite sar tae (hungry)
ဗိုက်အောင့်တယ်	bite aungt tae (stomachache)
အိုက်တယ်	eite tae (to feel hot)
လိုက်မလား။	Lite ma larr? (Will you come with me?)
ရှမ်းခေါက်ဆွဲကြိုက်လား။	Shann khout sweh kyite larr? (Do you like Shan noodles?)
ဓာတ်ပုံရိုက်လို့ရလား။	Dat p'own yite loht ya larr? (Can I take a photo?)
သူခွေးကိုက်ခံရတယ်။	Thu khwayy kite khan ya tae. (S/he was bitten by a dog.)
ဆိုင်	sai (shop)

စားသောက်ဆိုင်	sarr thout sai (restaurant)
လက်ဖက်ရည်ဆိုင်	let phet yi sai (teashop)
ပိုင်ရှင်	pai shin (owner)
ထိုင်းနိုင်ငံ	thaii nai ngan (Thailand)
စပျစ်ဝိုင်	sa pyit wai (Burmese grape wine)
ရှိုင်းတယ်	yaii tae (rude)
ရခိုင်ပြည်နယ်	ya khai pyi nae (Rakhine State)
ရန်ကုန်တိုင်းဒေသကြီး	yan kone taii day tha kyee (Yangon Region)
ကွမ်း	konn (betel nut)
လွမ်းတယ်	lwann tae (to miss someone/something)
မွန်ပြည်နယ်	mon pyi nae (Mon State)
ကွန်ရက်	kon yet (network)
ဇွန်းရှိလား။	Zonn sheet larr? (Do you have a spoon?)
လမ်းညွှန်	lann nhyon (guide, directory)
ဟွန်းမတီးပါနဲ့။	Honn ma tee par naet. (Please don't use your horn)
ခွန်အား	khon arr (strength)
ယွန်း	yonn (lacquer)
ပွတ်တယ်	put tae (rub)
ဘွတ်ဖိနပ်	but pheet nat (boots)
မွတ်ဆလင်	mut sa lin (Muslim)
ရေမွှေးဆွတ်တယ်	yay mwayy sut tae (to put on perfume)
အထွတ်အမြတ်	a htut a myat (holy)
တာယာကွျတ်	tar yar kyut (tire tube)
ချွတ်တယ်	chut tae (to take off)
ခွင့်လွှတ်တယ်	khwint hlut tae (to forgive)
အလွတ်တမ်းသတင်းထောက်	a lut tann tha tinn htout (freelance journalist)

Part

Reading and Writing Practice

In this part of the book you'll find a variety of reading and writing exercises that will help reinforce and consolidate your knowledge of the Burmese alphabet. The sections are divided into useful everyday topics, ranging from daily expressions, numbers and food to computers and social media.

🎧 GUIDED WRITING PRACTICE

Practice tracing the daily expressions, then try writing by yourself. Practice pronunciation using the online audio file.

1. Mingalarpar.   Hello.

    မင်္ဂလာပါ။

2. Nay kaungg larr?   How are you?

    နေကောင်းလား။

3. Kaungg tae.   Fine.

    ကောင်းတယ်။

4. Di lo bar beh.   So so.

    ဒီလိုပါပဲ။

5. Thate ma kaungg boo.   Not very well.

    သိပ်မကောင်းဘူး ။

6. Ta tar.   Goodbye.

    တာ့တာ။

7. Nout mha twayt mae naw.   See you later.

    နောက်မှတွေ့မယ်နော်။

8. Kaungg thaww nya par.   Goodnight.

    ကောင်းသောညပါ။

9. Kyayy zoo tin par tae.   Thank you.

    ကျေးဇူးတင်ပါတယ်။

10. Nan mae bae lo khaw leh?   What's your name?

နာမည်ဘယ်လိုခေါ်လဲ။ ....

11. Kyon tawt nan mae ka...par.   My name is... [male speaker]

ကျွန်တော့်နာမည်က...ပါ။ ....

12. Kyon ma nan mae ka...par.   My name is... [female speaker]

ကျွန်မနာမည်က...ပါ။ ....

13. Kha na layy naw.   Just a moment, please.

ခဏလေးနော်။ ....

14. Hote tae.   Yes! / That's right.

ဟုတ်တယ်။ ....

15. Bar mha, ma hote par boo.   No. / Nothing.

ဘာမှမဟုတ်ပါဘူး။ ....

16. Ma theet boo.   I don't know.

မသိဘူး။ ....

17. Tit sate lout.   Excuse me [polite].

တစ်ဆိတ်လောက်။ ....

18. Ya par tae.   That's all right. / It's okay.

ရပါတယ်။ ....

19. Kate sa, ma sheet par boo.   No problem.

ကိစ္စမရှိပါဘူး။ ....

🎧 GUIDED WRITING PRACTICE

Practice tracing then writing the spelled out number on the left and the Burmese figure on the right. Practice pronunciation using the online audio file.

1 (tit) တစ် ....

၁ ....

2 (nhit) နှစ် ....

၂ ....

3 (thownn) သုံး ....

၃ ....

4 (layy) လေး ....

၄ ....

5 (ngarr) ငါး ....

၅ ....

6 (chout) ခြောက် ....

၆ ....

7 (khoot nit) ခုနစ် ....

၇ ....

8 (shit) ရှစ် ....

၈ ....

9 (koh) ကိုး ....

၉ ....

10 (tit sae) တစ်ဆယ် ....

၁၀ ....

11 (saet tit) ဆယ့်တစ် ....

၁၁ ....

12 (saet nhit) ဆယ့်နှစ် ....

၁၂ ....

Reading Practice

Cover page 84 and see if you can match the spelled-out number to its meaning. Then write the Burmese figure for each number. Check your answers by referring to page 84.

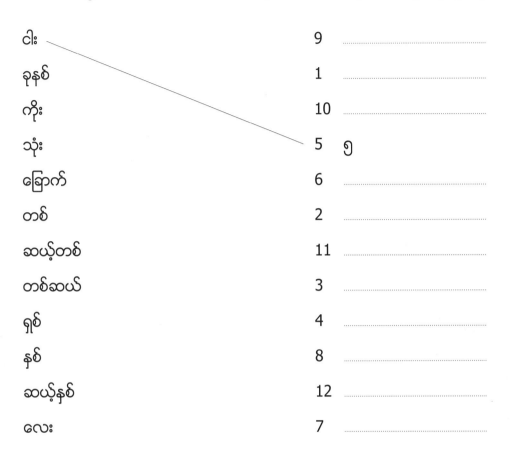

ငါး	9	
ခုနစ်	1	
ကိုး	10	
သုံး	5	၅
ခြောက်	6	
တစ်	2	
ဆယ့်တစ်	11	
တစ်ဆယ်	3	
ရှစ်	4	
နှစ်	8	
ဆယ့်နှစ်	12	
လေး	7	

🎧 LISTENING PRACTICE

Read and listen to the following phrases and underline the numbers. Check your answers on page 96.

1. ကိုးနာရီပါ။   Koh nar yi par.
   It's 9 o'clock.

2. လေးနာရီထိုးဖို့ ဆယ်မိနစ်   Layy nar yi htoh phoht, sae meet nit
   ten to four

3. နိုဝင်ဘာလ ၃ ရက်နေ့၊ ဗုဒ္ဓဟူးနေ့   november la, thownn yet nayt, bote da hoo nayt
   Wednesday 3 November

🎧 Match each word in the box to its Myanglish pronunciation, and write the word in the correct place. Once you have checked your answers on page 96, practice pronouncing the words using the online audio.

a)	သံရုံး	i)	ရဲစခန်း
b)	ဘုရား	j)	စာတိုက်
c)	ဈေး	k)	ဘူတာ
d)	ဆေးရုံ	l)	စားသောက်ဆိုင်
e)	ဘဏ်	m)	စာကြည့်တိုက်
f)	ဘတ်စ်ကားမှတ်တိုင်	n)	ဘား
g)	ဆေးဆိုင်	o)	ရုပ်ရှင်ရုံ
h)	ဟိုတယ်	p)	ပန်းခြံ

1. sar tite   post office

2. than y'ownn   embassy

3. sar kyeet tite   library

4. ho tae   hotel

5. zayy   market

6. sarr thout sai   restaurant

7. pann chan   park

8. ban   bank

9. sayy y'own   hospital

10. sayy sai   pharmacy

11. yote shin y'own   cinema

12. bu tar   train station

13. bus karr mhat tai   bus stop

14. barr   bar

15. yeh sa khann   police station

16. bootyarr   pagoda

🎧 GUIDED WRITING PRACTICE

Practice reading, tracing and writing the words below. Practice pronunciation with the audio file.

1. bats karr   bus

   ဘတ်စ်ကား

2. tet ka si   taxi

   တက္ကစီ

3. karr   car

   ကား

4. site karr   trishaw

   ဆိုက်ကား

5. tote tote   tuk tuk

   တုတ်တုတ်

6. set bee   bicycle

   စက်ဘီး

7. sai kae   motorcycle

   ဆိုင်ကယ်

8. hlay   boat

   လှေ

9. thin baww   ship

   သင်္ဘော

10. ya htarr   train

    ရထား

11. lay yin   airplane

    လေယာဉ်

Reading and Writing Practice

Label the pictures with words from the box. Check your answers by referring to page 88.

ဘတ်စ်ကား   တက္ကစီ   ကား   စက်ဘီး   ဆိုင်ကယ်   သင်္ဘော   ရထား   လေယာဉ်

1. ....

2. ....

3. ....

4. ....

5. ....

6. ....

7. ....

8. ....

■ A MYANMAR MENU ■

🎧 Match each menu item to its Myanglish pronunciation, and write the word in the correct place. Check your answers on page 96.

Breakfast

a) ကြက်ဥမွှေကြော်	c) အုန်းနို့ခေါက်ဆွဲ	e) ကြက်ဥပလာတာ
b) မုန့်ဟင်းခါး	d) ထမင်းကြော်	

1. m'ownt hinn kharr mohinga: fish and rice noodle soup ....

2. kyet oot pa lar tar fried flatbread with egg ....

3. ownn noht khout sweh coconut noodles ....

4. hta minn kyaw fried rice ....

5. kyet oot mhway kyaw omelet ....

Curries

a) ဘဲဥဟင်း	c) ကြက်သားဟင်း	e) ပုစွန်ဟင်း
b) ငါးဟင်း	d) အမဲသားဟင်း	f) ဝက်သားဟင်း

1. kyet tharr hinn   chicken curry

2. beh oot hinn   duck egg curry

3. wet tharr hinn   pork curry

4. ngarr hinn   fish curry

5. a meh tharr hinn   beef curry

6. poot son hinn   prawn curry

Salads

a) ဂျင်းသုပ်	c) မြင်းခွာရွက်သုပ်	e) ခေါက်ဆွဲသုပ်
b) လက်ဖက်သုပ်	d) ခရမ်းချဉ်သီးသုပ်	f) ထမင်းသုပ်

1.   let phet thote   tea leaf salad

2.   hta minn thote   rice salad

3.   kha yann chin thee thote   tomato salad

4.   khout sweh thote   noodle salad

5.   gyinn thote   ginger salad

6.   myinn khwar ywet thote   pennywort salad

Drinks

a)	ရေနွေးကြမ်း	c)	သံပုရာရည်	e)	ကော်ဖီမစ်
b)	ဖရဲသီးဖျော်ရည်	d)	လက်ဖက်ရည်	f)	သရက်သီးဖျော်ရည်

1. let phet yi   Burmese tea ....

2. yay nwayy kyann   green tea ....

3. kaw phi mit   instant coffee ....

4. than pa yar yi   lime juice ....

5. tha yet thee phyaw yi   mango juice ....

6. pha yeh thee phyaw yi   watermelon juice ....

 GUIDED WRITING PRACTICE

Practice reading, tracing and writing the words below. Practice pronunciation with the audio file.

1. kon pyu tar   computer

    ကွန်ပျူတာ

2. wai phai   Wi-Fi

    ဝိုင်ဖိုင်

3. letp tawt   laptop

    လက်ပ်တော့

4. in tar net   Internet

    အင်တာနက်

5. laii   connection

    လိုင်း

6. ee mayyl   email

    အီးမေးလ်

7. ee mayyl late sar   email address

    အီးမေးလ်လိပ်စာ

8. so shae mi di yar   social media

    ဆိုရှယ်မီဒီယာ

9. phayts but   Facebook

    ဖေ့စ်ဘွတ်

10. in sa tar ga ran   Instagram

    အင်စတာဂရမ်

11. etp   app

အက်ပ် ....

12. konn mant   comment
ကွန်းမန့် ....

13. met sayt   message
မက်ဆေ့ ....

14. sae phi   selfie
ဆယ်ဖီ ....

LISTENING AND READING PRACTICE

Read and listen to the sentences and underline the words to do with Internet and social media from the list above. Check your answers on page 96.

1. ဒီမှာ ဝိုင်ဖိုင်အလကားရလား။
   Is there free Wi-Fi here?

2. အီးမေးလ်လိပ်စာလေးပေးပါ။
   What is your email address?

3. ကျွန်တော့်ကို အီးမေးလ်ပို့လိုက်ပါလား။
   Could you send me an email?

4. လိုင်းကျတယ်။
   The Internet connection is slow.

5. ဆယ်ဖီဆွဲရအောင်။
   Let's take a selfie.

6. ဖေ့စ်ဘွတ်မှာ အက်ဒ်ပေးပါ။
   Add me on Facebook.

7. ဖေ့စ်ဘွတ်အကောင့်ရှိလား။
   Do you have a Facebook account?

8. ဒီဘာသာပြန်အက်ပလီကေးရှင်းရှိလား။
   Do you have this translation app?

🎧 Reading and Writing Sentences

Test your reading and writing skills by studying the word list below and then trying to read the text. Although you may be unfamiliar with Burmese grammar, you should be able to recognize and pronounce many of the words in the text. Use the audio file to help you. Once you feel confident that you can read the text with understanding, try writing the text out in the space below.

Vocabulary

ကျွန်မ = I, my (female speaker)

နာမည် = name

အသက် = age

နှစ် = year

မှာ = in, at (comes after time or place)

ပါ = polite particle (comes after noun or verb)

တယ် = ending particle after present tense verb

မယ် = ending particle after future tense verb

Noun + တွေ = plural form

Noun + နဲ့ = with, and, by

မေလ = May

တနင်္လာနေ့ = Monday

ဒီနေ့ = today

မနက်ဖြန် = tomorrow

မွေးနေ့ = birthday

ရွှေတိဂုံဘုရား = Shwedagon Pagoda

ပုဂံ = Bagan

စားသောက်ဆိုင် = restaurant

သူငယ်ချင်း = friend

ထမင်းကြော် = fried rice

လက်ဖက်ရည် = tea

နေ = to live, to stay

သွား = to go

မွေး = to be born

စား = to eat

သောက် = to drink

ကျွန်မနာမည် နီဒီပါ။ အသက် ၂၅ နှစ်ရှိပြီ။ ရန်ကုန်မှာ နေတယ်။ မေလ ၉ ရက်နေ့၊ တနင်္လာနေ့မှာ မွေးတယ်။ ဒီနေ့ ကျွန်မမွေးနေ့ပါ။ ရွှေတိဂုံဘုရားသွားမယ်။ စားသောက်ဆိုင်မှာ သူငယ်ချင်းတွေနဲ့ ထမင်းကြော်စားမယ်။ လက်ဖက်ရည်သောက်မယ်။ မနက်ဖြန် ပုဂံသွားမယ်။

Answer Key

Page 15

1. sa - စ
2. ga - ဂ
3. za - ၛ
4. kha - ခ
5. nya - ည
6. ka - ကြ
7. nga - င
8. ga - ဃ
9. sa - ဆ
10. za - ဇ

Page 25

1. nya - ည
2. ya - ရ
3. kha - ခ
4. ma - မ
5. hta - ထ
6. tha - သ
7. ta - တ
8. na - န
9. ah - အ
10. la - လ
11. pa - ပ
12. ka - က

Page 85

1. ကိုးနာရီပါ။
2. လေးနာရီထိုးဖို့ ဆယ်မိနစ်
3. နိုဝင်ဘာလ ၃ ရက်နေ့၊ ဗုဒ္ဓဟူးနေ့

Page 87

1. j
2. a
3. m
4. h
5. c
6. l
7. p
8. e
9. d
10. g
11. o
12. k
13. f
14. n
15. i
16. b

Page 90

1. b
2. e
3. c
4. d
5. a

Page 91 (curries)

1. c
2. a
3. f
4. b
5. d
6. e

Page 91 (salads)

1. b
2. f
3. d
4. e
5. a
6. c

Page 92

1. d
2. a
3. e
4. c
5. f
6. b

Page 94

1. ဒီမှာ ဝိုင်ဖိုင်အလကားရလား။
2. အီးမေးလ်လိပ်စာလေးပေးပါ။
3. ကျွန်တော့်ကို အီးမေးလ်ပို့လိုက်ပါလား။
4. လိုင်းကျတယ်။
5. ဆယ်ဖီဆွဲရအောင်။
6. ဖေ့စ်ဘွတ်မှာ အက်ဒ်ပေးပါ။
7. ဖေ့စ်ဘွတ်အကောင့်ရှိလား။
8. ဒီဘာသာပြန်အက်ပလီကေးရှင်းရှိလား။